# "PASS IT ON!"

*Love, Leelas & Lessons from*
## *Sathya Sai Baba*

# "PASS IT ON!"

## Love, Leelas & Lessons from
### *Sathya Sai Baba*

Karen Gill

Cover Photo: Jarrel Cudjoe

*Dedicated with love
to people everywhere
in pursuit of the
ultimate Truth*

# TABLE OF CONTENTS

# Introduction

*"It does not matter a bit if you have no faith in Me or God. Have faith in yourselves, that is enough. For who are you really? Each one of you is Divinity, whether you know it or not...Man must know his pricelessness...he should note that he is the imperishable Atma (divine consciousness) and the body is only a vehicle for Atma."*
- Sathya Sai Baba

Okay, I've got to make one thing clear from the get-go. I never intended to write about my relationship with or the impact of Sathya Sai Baba in my life. Only Michael, my husband, and at times our children and a small number of 'Baba friends' have been aware of His personal involvement over the past thirty-eight years. It's always been hard for me to share what's really personal. When it comes to Baba, I don't even know how to begin because He's given me the most profound, life-altering experiences of my life. Some of them have been miraculous and what I've gained from all of them together has skyrocketed the quality of my life. It's just my nature, though, to keep it all close to the vest.

Since elementary school my classmates gravitated to me to resolve their dilemmas. They confided in me for answers. Wisdom may or may not have been my long suit, but confidence certainly was. Right or wrong, my (implied) sage advice provided them solutions. It never crossed my mind to open up to them for any reason. That's just not me. Looking back I can see more than a few similarities to Charles Schulz' Peanut character, Lucy... but I've got a kinder heart and an Italian heritage.

Along the same vein, I feel social media involves way too much sharing. To me, it's invasive; it hooks you and I don't like it and I don't do it. When I'm visiting Sarah, my daughter in California, just enjoying a delicious cup of Philz coffee together, I don't need eighty people to know about it and 'like' it; *it's nobody's business!* I mention this only to help give a sense of the emotional backdrop here.

When Baba emphatically instructed me to "Pass it on!" almost two decades ago, I had no clue as to what He was *really* asking of me or how far out of my comfort zone it would take me, but I wanted to honor His request. Initially I thought that sharing some of the highlights of almost forty years of experiences with Him in a book would be fairly straight-forward, certainly not something that would take decades to accomplish. I'd simply be passing on the joy and wisdom I've derived from having Baba in my life, right? Well, it didn't take long to hit two possibly insurmountable obstacles. First, how do I find the right words when experiences with Baba often defy description? Our language isn't superlative enough or full enough and I don't have any formal training in writing. I heard an analogy once, "that trying to describe experiences with divinity is like trying to describe the word 'sweet' to a person who has never tasted sugar". It's actually even harder than that.

The second and even more intimidating hurdle is that I have to reveal the context, show where I was emotionally and spiritually when He intervened for the scope of His love and joy to be appreciated. *NO! I don't do that!* I really don't have the need or inclination to let the world see my spiritual challenges and growth... or lack thereof. Will this 'sharing' highlight my finer moments? I don't think so. After years and considerable effort trying to put experiences on paper without really opening up, I came to the conclusion that a research-style objective approach isn't going to work if I'm going to accomplish what Baba wants me to do. Talk about vulnerability...risk...oh God, the aahjida! What a mine-field for ego and image!

Sathya Sai Baba's reach is world-wide and often what He gives is life-altering (something most people gladly share). Over the last few decades I'd guess at least a hundred books have been written about Him, most quite eloquently by experienced authors from all around the globe. Many of them have spent a significant amount of time in Baba's physical presence, garnering blessings and wisdom from their proximity to Him. That wouldn't be me. Although I've travelled to His ashrams in India more than a half dozen times since 1989, our relationship has been less orthodox, but no less potent. How does one capture in words the inexpressible joy Baba gives? I think it would be easier to capture the Aurora Borealis! Please bear with me. I'm giving this task my best shot only because Baba has asked me to and as Michael pointed out, "He wouldn't have asked you if you *couldn't* do it!"

So, if I can squash my hefty ego and plow through my ineptitude, I'll share with you this personal glimpse and perhaps you, too, may want to claim this incomparable precious treasure known as Sathya Sai Baba.

# Chapter 1

## Baba 'Dreams'

*When I appear in a dream it is to communicate something to the individual. It is not a mere dream as is generally known. Do not think that these incidents...are stretches of your imagination.*
-Sathya Sai Baba

This is just one of the unconventional ways Baba sometimes intervenes to help. I have to admit, I'd be highly skeptical if it hadn't happened to me but it did. The beginning of a personal relationship with Sai Baba started in 1981 when He began 'visiting' me in my dream state. These visits are called Baba dreams but in my opinion they're not actually dreams at all. There's a different quality to them. They're more vivid and somehow more real than normal waking life. After experiencing a Baba dream it's as if this 'normal' worldly plane of existence is the sometimes fuzzy, illogical, disconnected dream state. All *THIS*, everyday life, can seem like the Mad Hatter's tea party! In a way, the contrast makes it a little easier to accept that dreams with

Him are not concocted by my mind, that they're given as gifts by Him and have a significant point to make.

Although I'll be sharing conversations between us, the fullness and purity of the energy that imbues them might be beyond my scope to translate into words. As I already mentioned, when it comes to Baba, words often can't say enough to accurately depict the experience. There's too much to recount all the topics He's addressed over the decades. So, in looking back through almost forty years of dream journals, I've picked out some that I hope might resonate with you too. But first, here's a quick synopsis of what led up to the first Baba dream in my life.

Long story short, in 1981 I found myself standing next to a stranger who had a small picture of Baba on a key ring she was holding in her hand. Although I'd never seen His image before, there was something so familiar about Him; it was in the eyes. I asked who He was and she briefly explained and a few days later I was given a copy of <u>Sai Baba</u>, <u>Man</u> <u>of</u> <u>Miracles</u> by Howard Murphet. What an eye-opener! The whole book is filled with accounts from people all over the world who've had experiences with Baba that would be considered miraculous, not humanly possible. It became clear that He is not bound by our normal known laws of Physics. Sometimes His manifestations seem normal, because they happen so often and with so little fanfare. Baba says it's His Sankalpa, divine will, and He considers His gifts of miracles to be His calling cards; that when He gives people what they think they want, they're more likely to sit up and take notice and will hopefully one day want what He's truly come to give. Much has been written about it but His mission is simple: to help us realize our inherent divinity (experience it) and to show how we can align our thoughts, words and actions to remove selfish egotistical behavior we've acquired, which covers up that divine essence.

I couldn't stop thinking about Baba after finishing the book. Many of His miracles resemble those of Jesus – healings, manifestations, the raising of the dead and more. Is it possible that a spiritual teacher of that caliber is on Earth *now*? Oh my God...and I'm here too...*OH-MY-GOD!!!* Not that His presence in the world was likely to have anything to do with my life, but yet... After all, He was half way around the world, incredibly busy in India helping millions of 'needy' people with all His humanitarian projects... but what a time to be alive on Earth! What hope!

Since my very first dream visit Baba has been showing me that He knows *everything* there is to know about me and all that's currently going on in my life, even my thoughts, right down to the most miniscule hope and fear. Nothing needs to be explained; He knows what makes me tick and has my spiritual blueprint, complete with all the 'growth' opportunities I still need to take on in this life. With His guidance and apparently never-ending patience, over the years I have grown in wisdom and it's allowed me to occasionally stoke my inner divine spark into a roaring blaze. (Yesss!) Not that I'm a 'roaring blaze' on a daily basis... but life is so much happier and full and more peaceful and the persistent anguish from a deep sense of separation I've felt since adolescence is gone. Even though the remedy I craved was out there, going through most of my teenage years in the '60's in Auburn, New York, there was no one in my family to point me in the right direction to find what I needed. It took more than a decade of searching before I heard the term 'spiritual yearning' and realized that this is what I'd been suffering from. Sorry, I'm getting ahead of myself.

Whether a person has Baba dreams or not, most who have experienced Him in any way often feel they have a special connection to Him. What's most surprising to me is that this connection can be made *no matter which plane it comes from*. Baba released His physical form for this life in 2011 but that fact makes no difference at all in my life. He's just as alive and involved with me without a physical body on Earth. He still provides everything I need through His dreams and boons and leelas. His

Presence and guidance hasn't changed one iota. Omnipresent and omniscient, along with the heart-stopping purity and power of His love is what I envision God to be but please know that sharing my experiences with Him is not to convince anybody of anything. If you're open to the possibility that your perception of reality can actually be vastly greater than you thought, and you have a yearning to find what's real, then you're likely to see how much Baba can enrich and elevate life here on Earth. My new-found clarity from His spiritual perspectives is stunning, as though I've switched from living in a black & white silent movie to Technicolor and Dolby surround sound!

One aspect of Baba's dream visits that differs from normal dreams is that He creates many different kinds of relationships between us, depending on what it takes to get through to me at the time. He may be my life-long very best friend, and I'm light-hearted and delighted to see Him. Then there's a more serious, professor-style formality, where I'm the student and need to sit up, pay attention and get in gear. A couple of times He's popped in as my physician. At the other end of the spectrum, thankfully rare, if I'm embroiled in something where I'm really off-track spiritually, Baba can appear formidably powerful and devastatingly aloof and He ignores me, withholding His natural outpouring of love. The separation between us is gut-wrenchingly painful and forces me back to waking consciousness, usually in tears.

Out of all of His dream visits, my favorite, hands down, is when we're in close proximity and I can feel myself actually absorb His radiance, His exquisite, blissful love and light. In that moment the absolute perfection and purity that IS Sathya Sai Baba is also fully in me. All desires, as well as speech, motion and time disappear. Perfect equilibrium and unshakeable deep peace pervades everything.

The spiritual wisdom He imparts may sound familiar, as it is the foundation of many major religions, but without the dogma. With Baba, instead of arbitrary rules to blindly follow (which, in some cases, have been inspired by politics instead of spirituality), it's more like I'm being given the perfect recipe for exactly what I want to create. He also helps me create it by working by my side in the kitchen, giving little tips that can make a huge difference in the outcome. So, to begin, the following are a few Baba dream visits on a variety of topics.

April, 1986 – I was among hundreds of other people in a large room and all of them, including myself, had no bones! We were all smushed faces, limbs, disgusting-looking jellyfish-like blobs with eyes puddled on the floor. Frantically looking around I could see that most people weren't even concerned about this condition let alone panicked. What was going on? I knew Baba was in the room somewhere and He would know. With great effort I managed to shift and slide myself along the floor, maneuvering carefully around others until I finally found Him. When I asked what happened to everybody He explained that it was people's continual selfish desires that made them sink so low. Constantly satisfying mundane, material desires had rendered us all 'spineless'. We had little control, no self-discipline over our senses anymore. It was sad; how could we discover our own divinity and achieve liberation? With that thought I immediately decided to change it for myself. As I sensed this resolute determination, my spine suddenly started growing and within seconds grew to almost three feet tall... then it stopped. Standing next to Baba I sighed with an enormous wave of hope. He, of course was at His full height. Maybe now that I know, I'll get to my full height too, although I realized that *wanting* to improve could only take me so far.

Spring, 1985 – Preface: I'd 'known' Baba for about three years and had made several changes in my life to become more aligned with His spiritual teachings. On the whole I thought I was doing a pretty good job and was feeling quite close to Him.

In this dream I was seated in a large packed auditorium with the lights already turned down waiting for a play to begin. Suddenly a flurry of excited whispers caught my attention. Baba had arrived unexpectedly and had taken a seat in the audience about three or four rows behind me and several seats over to the right. How exciting! I was so close but still, just *had* to get closer to Him. I seriously considered climbing over the rows of filled seats to get to Him but knew that would not be acceptable and the rows were too long for me to make my way to the end and go around. Hugely disappointed, I resigned myself to the fact that from where I was sitting, it wasn't possible to get any closer. When the play was over I was among a few dozen other devotees waiting backstage for Baba in the green room. He was quickly ushered in followed by an entourage and He spotted me and made His way directly to me. Smiling and clearly happy to see me, I was thrilled but couldn't help notice as He approached that He was only two feet tall! Instantly dropping to my knees, we hugged. It was a big, best-friend-in-the-world, long-time-no-see kind of hug. Then it was over. As I awoke, the strong impression I was left with was that sometimes you have to be down on your knees to be up to Baba's stature. It wasn't something I'd given any thought to, but I couldn't say that humility has ever been my long suit...

February, 1992 – Preface: This visitation addressed two separate issues. Lying in bed, about to fall asleep, an idea popped in my head about becoming an 'owner/donor' of a room in

Baba's ashram. Imagining how nice and efficiently it could be fixed up with all the comforts of home, I drifted off to sleep.

In this dream there were two large adjacent gymnasiums for people to wait for Baba to come and give His blessing (darshan). The first room had bright spotlights overhead, which were aimed on long cafeteria-style tables. Lots of people had brought along big portable coolers filled with refreshments for their convenience and had lined them up on the tables. It seemed like a pretty good idea to have what they might want readily available. However, I couldn't help but notice that the atmosphere in the room was that of a social picnic-type gathering and people were chatting. No one seemed focused on Baba. The second adjoining room had no tables, coolers or spotlights and it was quiet. Without the social atmosphere and distractions I could already feel Baba's presence in that space even though He hadn't physically arrived yet. Instinctively it was obvious that this is where He would enter first and it wouldn't be crowded and I'd have a much better darshan, so it was where I wanted to be. (So much for fixing up a room in the ashram 'with all the comforts of home'!)

The scene shifted and Baba descended a flight of stairs into the room where I was waiting. Uncharacteristically, He didn't look happy or smile at me. He carried a puppy but it wasn't cute and handed it over to me without any joy or warmth, announcing, "It's yours." I was surprised and unsure what to do with it. I didn't want it and there was no good place to keep it and it was clearly inappropriate to have where I was.

Afterthought: when I woke up the next morning, I recalled that a dog can symbolically represent anger. In my normal waking life I'd recently become very angry at a friend who'd taken a trip to Baba in India. She'd agreed to take a package (which I'd *so* carefully put together) for a child I sponsored through the Christian Children's Fund. I knew someone in India she could give it to who was willing to personally deliver it to the remote village where the child lived. As it turned out, space in her suitcase was tight so she didn't take it and had her husband mail it back to me about a month later. I was furious. She totally failed in my expectation of her as a friend. She said she'd take it and she didn't! It meant a lot to me to have the family receive these gifts yet the mail had proven unreliable in the past. Here, Baba showed me that not only was He aware of what had happened, but that I needed to 'own' and deal with this 'dog' of temper. Not that I condone my behavior, but I did take note that it was a puppy instead of a full-grown dog.

August, 1996 – In this dream I was sitting cross-legged on the floor of Baba's interview room. The lighting was low and Baba sat in front, facing a small group of us. Unexpectedly, He stood up, walked to the back of the room and selected a neatly folded, dark colored, heavy wool blanket, which He presented as a gift to an elderly woman in the room. As He handed it to her, our eyes met and impulsively I asked Him (telepathically) if He would give me a gift, too. It didn't matter what it was; it just needed to be personally from Him, specifically for me, something solid I could hold onto. I held my breath while He stared at me intently, apparently analyzing something in His mind. In a silent, awkward moment I knew that He'd come to the conclusion that I would not also receive a blanket. Instead, He chose a large, round, ivory colored satin curtain tie-back. It was huge for a tie-back, more than six inches in diameter, with foot-long tassels dangling from it. It reminded me of something you might see in a large old Victorian style mansion with very high ceilings and enormous windows. I was appreciative and accepted it graciously but had absolutely no clue as to why He would give that to me. You know the saying, "You can't see the forest for the trees."? It took me several years to figure this out and it's so simple. What does a tie-back do? It eliminates the darkness and limited view that a curtain creates. So my 'gift' is an instrument to help dispel darkness and bring in more light!

October, 1984 – Preface: Here's another example of why you ought to write down your Baba dream immediately if you have one. The symbology is obvious in hindsight but again, it took many years before the light bulb went on.

I was among a fairly large group of people standing inside an airy foyer of a white marble building. Darshan was over but I knew that if I could get upstairs to Baba's private residence, there was a good chance I'd be able to ask Him about something important. The only issue was that the general public wasn't permitted there. I didn't let that deter me. Somehow I managed to scoot up the winding staircase unobtrusively. At the top of the steps there were several massive white columns in a spacious living area. I caught a glimpse of Baba hurrying off in another direction. Quickly running over to Him, I blurted out my question, "Baba, what do You want me to do to help?" Initially He looked surprised to see me, but then with a serious, no-nonsense attitude He replied, "You want to help? Come with Me." He led the way through a long dimly lit corridor that eventually opened up to the backstage of a very large theatre. Without pausing, He continued out onto the well-lit stage and walked directly over to a three-legged stool with a typed script sitting on it. Picking it up, He placed it firmly in my hands. "You want to help? Here! *THIS* is what I want you to do!" I had no idea what He was talking about. Was I supposed to direct a play? Be an actor in one? Suddenly I was sitting way up in the balcony looking down at the stage and noticed two rows of people filling seats in the front orchestra section. I knew that whatever this was, it wouldn't be ready to go on stage for a long time, but some were already waiting for it. A thought popped into my mind. *These must be the people who really need to hear what I have to say.* That was the end of the dream. Years later, the realization finally struck me that it wasn't a script Baba handed over to me; it was the *manuscript about US that I had yet to write!*

July, 1996 – It was only the two of us. I was Baba's helper in the kitchen and it was a *wonderful* working relationship! Baba prepared all the food and plated it and I served it to everyone who came to the dining hall. I noticed that these people did not look financially needy. At one point Baba filled four special dishes and asked me to deliver them to the pundits. Their meals were a little different from the others and they each had more on the plate, too. I passed them out to where they needed to go. The pundits stood out because their style of dress distinguished them from everyone else. Shortly after delivering their food, all four called me over and handed their plates back to me to return to the kitchen. Only a tiny portion had been eaten. That surprised me. They didn't accept what Baba personally 'dished out' to them? Aren't these people supposed to be the 'best' and able to take the most? They'd all just picked around the edges. Baba clearly noticed how much of what He'd given them that hadn't been touched. I could see that He wasn't happy about it and didn't approve of their decisions but He didn't comment on it. We finished up in the kitchen. It was hard work but invigorating, and we both felt happy and energized from a sense of accomplishment that we were able to satisfy the hunger of all those who came. He removed His big white kitchen apron and gave me a hearty hug!

Afterthought: As I awoke from this dream the lesson was clear. Sometimes the designated 'higher' ones, with all their credentials, titled positions and distinguished attire, may not necessarily be the ones who actually take (on) the most. The bottom line is to not be intimidated by outward signs of spiritual superiority. Baba knows what we can handle and has prepared the appropriate plate for each of us. Accepting it or not is a personal choice. Comparing what I can offer to the experiences of other authors is a waste of time and my assessment may or may not be correct. It's a big lesson; insecurity about my ability to write this has plagued me from the beginning. *How do I relay the unimaginable joy to be had through Baba's love and involvement?* I'm not sure if I can do it adequately. Still, if you can also take in what I've discovered through our relationship (the spiritual sustenance from *my* kitchen) and it brings you a higher quality of life right now, too, it's worth me taking the risk of burning my soufflé or having it collapse from my inexperience.

The transformation that comes about when I absorb His wisdom puts me in a better place in every way. I've got to admit, though, it hasn't come easy. Instead of comfortably cruising along my spiritual highway or even plodding steadily up my imaginary spiritual ladder, my progression looks more like an Alaskan salmon thrashing its way upstream to spawning grounds. It hasn't escaped me, either, that Baba's dream visitations could be considered remedial tutoring for the good-hearted but hard-headed.

# Chapter 2

## In the Beginning

*"Life is granted to us by God to enable us to seek and attain God."*
A Compendium of the Teachings of Sathya Sai Baba, maxim #88

Despite my natural reluctance, I will share some of my background here to show how unlikely circumstances led me to Baba.

This life started in the early '50s in Auburn, a small city at the edge of Owasco Lake, one of the Finger Lakes in upstate New York. I'm one of several grandchildren of Loretta and Nicholas Mastroianni and Amadeo and Josephine Valentino. All four of my grandparents came to the United States from Italy in the early 1900s from two tiny villages in the mountains outside Naples. Like so many others at the time, they had little money, no college education and could barely speak English. However, they had hope for a better future and were willing to work hard for it. It wasn't easy, but they were frugal, intensely Catholic and they understood the importance of an education. When they had a family these traits were instilled in their children from an early age.

My mother grew up in Auburn and my father in New York City. They married in 1948 right after my mother's high school graduation and my father's discharge from the Navy. Five years after their marriage they settled in Auburn to start a family, where I grew up surrounded by my mother's side of the family.

I was rarely alone. Besides parents and grandparents and a younger sister and much younger brother, I had lots of other relatives. Through Mom's sisters there were three sets of aunts and uncles and six first cousins. Then there were the great aunts and a great uncle (Grampa's siblings) and their spouses who also had children and grandchildren, so there was an extended family of lots of second and third cousins, too. We all lived within about a ten minute drive from one another and got together often. My first cousins in Auburn were like brothers and sisters and we all knew we had to obey to our aunts just like we did our mother - or else! Uninvited advice was never in short supply and no one would ever be accused of diplomacy, but that's another story.

The only people close who were outside the family were my godparents. Aunt Vivienne was Mom's best friend since high school. When I was old enough to notice, I could see that my mother, always the person-in-charge, had sharp edges. Because of Aunt Viv's inherent motherly, nurturing spirit she just naturally made everyone around her feel good and comfortable and happy. She embodied what I instinctively felt 'home' should be. I didn't get to spend as much time as I would have liked with her but she was a light in my life. The point of mentioning the relatives around me is to make it clear that I didn't grow up in a setting prone to making me feel isolated; many good people were part of my childhood.

My parents couldn't afford to go to college but their innate intelligence and work ethic helped them both become very successful in business. My father owned Auburn Floor Covering for forty-six years, in downtown Auburn. Mom was a pioneer in her field and Auburn's only local female celebrity. She was 'discovered' when I was six years old and became the host of a public affairs radio show on WMBO, which was enormously popular for decades. She also grew with her involvement in American Women in Radio and Television, providing opportunities for international travel and interviews with nationally known figures. When cable television was brought to Auburn she accepted a new career opportunity and learned every aspect of the business. At the height of her career she was the President and CEO of Auburn Cablevision and became the first woman on the Board of the New York State

Cable Association. Quite an accomplishment for a woman in the '50's!

Outwardly both parents were extremely sociable and very involved with the public. Privately they were emotionally unavailable. It didn't appear that parenthood was fulfilling for either of them. My father hoped his first child would be a boy but he got me instead and almost four years later, my sister. His disappointment was obvious and his interest and patience with us very thin. Surprisingly, his attitude didn't improve when my brother came along eleven years after me.

The children in our family were never encouraged to express personal feelings of any kind. The only time I was ever asked how I felt was when I had the chicken pox, mumps and measles, but I don't think that was a factor. Expectations were made crystal clear at a very early age: Always show respect and shut-up when adults are in the room talking to each other. *Never* take the last piece of food on a serving plate. *Never* answer back. Do assigned household chores without complaint (or you'll get more) and, last but not least, study hard - or suffer consequences! It may sound harsh but I had nothing else to compare it to at the time. That was life. The rules may have been exacting but it didn't seem to be an issue.

On the flip side, my parents' success brought me significant material advantages that they didn't have growing up, including graduation from a four-year private college, and wonderful opportunities for travel here and abroad. To Mom's approval, after graduate work in economics, the first job I held living on my own was in Washington, D.C. as a research assistant in the Policy Analysis Department of American Petroleum Institute (API).

Moving to the opposite end of the emotional spectrum was Gramma Mastroianni and love just shined through her in a million little ways, creating a life-long impact on me. In the Italian culture, food is love. I can remember from elementary school, before my parents bought our large house on South Street, the upscale side of town, I'd walk to Gramma's house every day after school. She always kept a dish warm on the stove for me of whatever she'd made for lunch and lunchtime was their main meal of the day. Then sometimes she'd pull out the portable record player for us and put on an album of her favorite Italian songs. While she sang along with it, I would provide her with an enthusiastic extemporaneous dance performance, dramatically lunging and prancing around the kitchen, arms outstretched, expressively using all the available space. When the record and my performance finished she'd applaud for me and share her Lorna Doones from the super-secret hiding drawer. As a regular 'special treat' for both of us she'd also turn on TV from 4:00 to 4:30 (she was the only one with the authority to touch the dials) and we'd sit together to watch Make Room for Daddy. She just loved Danny Thomas and I just loved sitting next to her to watch it.

Out of everything she did, I think Gramma showed her love for us the most through her cooking. She had more patience than anyone else in the family and let me help her. The 'downstairs' kitchen is where all the big, messy jobs were done, from canning what came out of their garden, to making the sweet Italian specialties for the whole family at the holidays. It included an old industrial extra-large gas stove with huge burners and a good-sized sturdy white porcelain table to work on. Without even thinking about it, when Gramma worked in the downstairs kitchen, I felt she filled the air with goodness and a touch of excitement and anticipation.

For example, a simple snack, but somehow so much more when Gramma made pizza fritte, fried dough 'fingers' (an inch or so wide and about six inches long). After carefully turning the raw dough strips into golden snacking perfection, she'd stack a mountain of them in her massive porcelain bowl that was lined with a grocery bag cut open to soak up the excess oil. We, along with my aunts and first cousins would show up within a few minutes of getting her phone call to come over. Coming down the steps to the basement, you'd get the aroma of gently bubbling olive oil cooking the fresh dough intermingled with the pungency of Grampa's and Uncle Tony's wooden wine barrels. Their wines were red and strong. The door to the wine cellar was kept closed but it was right off the kitchen. Besides the pizza fritte, she'd often have a few cookie sheets of her home-made pizza popped in the oven, too. I'd watch her take them out when they were ready and cut them up into uniform squares for everybody, while the grownups were still engrossed in lively conversations. As soon as she set the cookie sheets on the table, we all went for our favorite, either an inside softer piece or a crusty edge, and devoured the fresh pizza along with the pizza fritte. I remember her contented smile as she saw all of her work vanish into our mouths. Hundreds of memories that still make me smile were made with Gramma in that downstairs kitchen.

A very different slice of childhood, also impactful, involved religion. Our Catholic Church and Jesus were not presented as a source of comfort or support. Actually, Father Nocca's prognosis for Catholic souls here on Earth was pretty bleak. Here's one example from when I was six and in the first grade. I'd had a religious instruction class at church to get ready to make my First Communion. Scared out of my wits, I remember racing out to my mother who was waiting for me in the car in the church parking lot. Panting from fear and having run as fast as I could, I shouted out to her pleading, "Mommy! I HAVE to go to Catholic school all the time! Father Nocca says if we all don't it's going to be a *mortal* sin and those are the worst and I might not be able to get rid of it and I might *BURN IN HELL FOREVER!*"

There was never any mention of "...behold the kingdom of God is within you" in our parish. It wasn't until I was a freshman in college with a Jewish roommate from Long Island that it was brought to my attention that I'd been raised 'old-school Catholic'. Our priest was unrelenting in his repetitious message. Although he changed up the delivery every now and then, the bottom line was always the same: You're born a sinner, you'll die a sinner and all you can do in-between is confess, repent, and pray to Jesus for mercy and forgiveness...because Jesus loves you. In an accusatory voice we were regularly reminded, "Jesus *died* for *YOUR* sins!" As a teenager, once, in a moment of angry defiance (and in an attempt to shake off the guilt) I remember yelling out in my mind to no one in particular: *I'm REALLY sorry Jesus died because of me but why is it MY fault? I didn't ASK Him to!*

Our religion dangled meek hope in front of us, even if the chances of success were between slim and none. *If* I followed *all* the Catholic rules, including but not limited to going to church every Sunday, confessing all my venial and mortal sins weekly and dropping the provided envelope with ten percent of my parents' salary into the roving basket, m-a-y-b-e-, through God's mercy, I might end up in heaven for eternity when I died (most likely *after* taking the not-so-scenic route through purgatory).

Not surprisingly, I stepped back from the church as soon as I could, in my mid teenage years when my mother's attendance slacked off after my younger sister made her Confirmation. I never deliberately stepped away from Jesus but whenever I thought of Him I always felt so guilty and bad about what He went through and uncertain of the role I played in it all. Even though I was told to pray to Him for forgiveness, I was pretty sure I didn't have the right to hope for a personal friendship. I knew He was exceptionally good (the son of God!) but something didn't add up if I was eventually going to be judged by Him and possibly end up in Hell.

Around the age of ten my general contentment in life started eroding, with an uneasy vague sense that something was missing. I couldn't identify what was missing, but I couldn't shake it. As time went on, it seemed crucial to find important answers, even though I didn't know what the important questions were. I envisioned a huge theatre with an enormous stage and a closed stage curtain. There was no doubt in my mind it was vitally important to get behind that curtain to find out what I was supposed to know so everything could be in order and  good. At that time, though, it was an impossible task because I didn't know where to find the theatre, let alone the curtain!

Over the next several years this state of mind intensified and morphed into a sense of loss and separation and often overwhelming loneliness. It was confusing and a little scary because it made no sense. I was surrounded by lots of good relatives and had friends at school, too, but I couldn't fend off what turned into this terrible homesickness that sometimes physically hurt inside my chest, to the point of tears. *How* could I be homesick? Who could I talk to about it? Absolutely no one. I never had the opportunity to be with Aunt Viv by myself and as I said, nobody ever talked about personal feelings in our house. It just wasn't done. I could easily imagine the irritated, curt reaction from my father. "You feel *separated? Homesick and sad? What the hell's the matter with you? You haven't gone anywhere! Cut it out!*"

From my perspective back then, religion didn't have anything to do with this and spirituality and philosophy were completely off my radar. No matter what else was going on, though, these underlying emotions were there.

It festered in college and finally specific questions erupted: *Who am I, really? Why am I here? What is the point? What am I not seeing that's SO important to know? What will make my homesickness stop? How can I fill up this void inside me?*

I had a close relationship with a couple of people in college, but still couldn't bring myself to talk to them about it. How could they understand? It was too personal and the worst part was that I couldn't justify these feelings. A normal person would think I was out of my mind and, whether it was true or not, I didn't want to give that impression. If there was even an inkling as to what was wrong, I might have an idea as to what to do about it. It took more than a decade of searching before discovering that all I'd been going through is not so uncommon after all and it actually has a name: Spiritual Yearning. Without realizing it at the time, I embarked on my own personal treasure hunt of 'Self-inquiry', years before noticing that my spiritual journey had already begun.

Something came up in the summer of 1971, just a few weeks before leaving home for college. I saw a flyer about a five-day intensive workshop called Silva Mind Control, which was being offered at our WMCA. I'd never heard of it and it looked intriguing so I signed up for it.

Using guided imagery techniques, we were shown how to lower the frequency of our brainwave pattern to the alpha level, a calm, meditative mental state, to become more sensitive to subtler energy. In one exercise my assigned partner gave me only the name, age and location of a person who had a physical ailment. He knew all the details of the problem but didn't share it with me at the beginning. Imagining myself in the special healing room that we'd all mentally constructed for this work, I could 'see' where in the body the problem was, which was later verified. More importantly, we were also shown how to mentally send focused healing energy to the person who needed it. I seemed to have a knack for it and have done it hundreds of times successfully, and besides pinpointing the problem, I usually see what the person actually looks like.

So, at the age of eighteen I came to the astounding discovery that I can not only 'see' and feel energy and energy abnormalities in a body, but that my individual *thoughts actually carry energy* and can make a positive difference! WOW! I couldn't tell you how it worked, but it worked! There is much more available to us than our five senses provide. Could this be a clue or connected to whatever I needed to find behind the curtain? I had no idea. Maybe it might lead to something else. Although I was familiar with the idea of the power of prayer, in the Catholic religion we're taught to petition Mary or a saint or even Jesus to intervene. As parishioners, we could pray for assistance, but we weren't given the option of intervening *ourselves* to help others. My directed *energy* can affect others? In 1971 this was big news to me! Now it's much more mainstream.

After grad school, when I lived on "P" Street in D.C., two places affected my world in a big way, a metaphysical bookstore in Georgetown called "YES!" and a Spiritualist church, The Church of Two Worlds. Granted, I was from a small town in upstate New York, BUT... an actual religion dedicated to proving the existence of life after death? I hadn't previously thought about it much (except for the whole Heaven/Hell idea, which just didn't sit right) so I wanted to check this out, especially after the eye-opening experience with the Silva course.

In one part of the Sunday service, the minister would give a specific, private message to a parishioner from a loved one who'd passed on. Several were given each week. The one thing they had in common was that they all contained specific information that only the intended receiver could have known. Observing people's reactions for more than a year, their surprise, sometimes shock and tears confirming the message's validity, I came to the conclusion that this degree of specificity and accuracy was beyond coincidence or anything that could have been made up.

My horizons widened further. According to this evidence-based doctrine, upon death, the soul (resident of the body) is NOT extinguished! (And *NOBODY* is going to burn in Hell *forever!...Did I have news for Father Nocca!)* When you die, the soul leaves the body but remains intact and unharmed and may still be available to us here on earth. Again, quite an eye-opener, and it's also connected to energy.

Surprisingly to me at first, making contact with a deceased loved one is not difficult to do and contrary to some mediums' shtick, there's nothing mystical or mysterious about it. It only takes clear intent and practice to tap into this frequency of communication. You can think of it as turning a dial on a radio to get a specific wavelength for different music on different stations. I didn't know exactly how this skill could be of use to me, but you never know, so I took advantage of the opportunity to become reasonably adept at it.

Between this and dozens of new authors I discovered through YES! Bookstore, a whole new world opened to me. I couldn't believe that I hadn't found out about all this before! Thanks to Ralph Waldo Emerson (Transcendentalism) and the theosophists and Edgar Cayce and Jane Roberts and dozens of others, I finally realized that I *wasn't crazy and I wasn't the only one* who's suffered from spiritual yearning! My torment since childhood has been happening to people all over the world for thousands of years! What a relief! All those years...I didn't know I'd been desperately craving the energy of God. For the first time in my life since it all began I had hope that my deep 'homesickness' would go away at some point. I only needed more pieces of the puzzle to figure out how.

No meaningful account of my life could be complete without including Michael, my husband. Even though I don't consider myself a writer, I could devote reams of pages to our relationship and adventures. However, that's not why you're here with this book in your hand. So I'll confine myself to just the beginning of the two of us together and his influence on my spiritual growth spurt.

There was a picture-perfect blue sky on that unseasonably warm Saturday in D.C. on March 5th of 1977. Spring seemed to have arrived in full force all in one day and it felt great! Donna, a friend and colleague at API, lived in the apartment building next to mine. As we often did on weekends, we planned to explore something new. That weekend I came up with the suggestion of going over to The Church of Two Worlds for a reading, something I'd recently found out they offered on Saturdays once a month. Her response was tepid but she agreed. "Alright... I'll give it a try. I'm not sure I buy into all that but it would be something new and different."

So we headed out to Georgetown to the church, a few minutes' bus ride away. Appointments could only be made in person on a first-come-first-served basis. They had a social hall where you could browse through books or purchase a sandwich while you waited for the reader you signed up for. We made our appointments and then found two empty folding chairs together at a long table which happened to be across from a man who seemed fully absorbed in eating an apparently scrumptious egg salad sandwich. I couldn't help but notice him and the first thought that went through my mind was *Hmmm...what a good eater!* That was very odd; I'd never made that sort of assessment of anyone before (or since) in my life.

He made an impressive sight, with strong broad shoulders, dark hair and a well-kempt beard (that didn't hide his perfectly round Santa-like cheeks when he smiled). As we sat down he lifted his attention from the sandwich and looked directly at me. His eyes took my breath away. They were a deep greyish blue, stunningly clear and emanated such a kind, loving spirit. I had the feeling he was seeing straight into my soul. It was unsettling but yet thrilling and comforting all at the same time. With a slight nod and smile he greeted us and introduced himself.

From that first hello I felt a strong sense of familiarity. Conversation was comfortable, almost as if we were catching up on things, reuniting after a long separation rather than beginning to get to know each other. Michael grew up in Silver Spring, Maryland, a suburb of D.C. and was five years older than me, we both have our birthdays in August and we're both the eldest of three children in our families and... there are a million details I could tell you but none of that matters. What IS significant is the discovery that his level of interest and enthusiasm in spiritual and metaphysical topics matched mine! He was 'looking', too! Delving into different philosophies and exchanging personal insights and being able to unreservedly ask questions was like finding an oasis in the desert!

The day after we met, the pews were packed in church for the Sunday service. Nevertheless, we both spotted each other in the crowd and smiled. I was hoping to connect with him again but when the service ended I didn't see him and couldn't stay long because I needed to catch the last bus back to Dupont Circle. He spotted me at the bus stop in front of the church and offered to drive me home. Perfect! There was no doubt that I could trust him, (sometimes you just *know)* so I immediately accepted.

Since it was fairly close by, before the service I'd stopped at Yes! Bookstore. Besides all the books and some records, they had a small bulk foods section, too. I'd picked up some whole wheat spaghetti, a fairly new phenomenon in 1977, which was loose in a brown paper bag, and I'd also bought a record of American Indian Healing Chants.

Walking together to his car, Michael told me that he'd just bought a used Falcon 500 that week. I explained that after paying a ridiculous amount of money for parking tickets and getting the 'boot' too, I'd taken my car back to Auburn to my parents' house. He accompanied me to the passenger side to open my door. It didn't budge. After several tries with no luck, he got into the driver's seat and reached over to try to open it from the inside. It still wouldn't budge. Embarrassed, he asked if I'd be willing to climb in through the driver's side. I didn't want him to feel any more uncomfortable so I downplayed it and quickly started to get in. It turned out to be trickier than I thought, between wearing a dress and climbing over the stick shift while holding on to my purse and the album and spaghetti...Before I could catch it, all the pasta came sliding out of the paper bag, onto the car seat and all over the floor! Although Michael's natural energy seemed quite calm and unruffled, he saw what was happening and was mortified. Immediately he called out, "Don't worry! I'll get it! I'll get it! Let me get that for you!" So I carefully backed out and he dove in to retrieve every strand and stuffed it all back into the brown bag and handed it over to me. In an attempt to reassure me he said, "It's okay. We can dust it off; you can still use it."

I looked at him in disbelief. He had no idea what those words did inside me. You see, another of my father's 'issues' had to do with germs. I remember furious outbursts and punishment if a serving platter on the dinner table was accidentally passed too close to his dish, potentially dropping germs (from clean dishes on a clean table?) onto his food. I looked at Michael's face, so innocently sincere and concerned... and adorable. From great depths, uncontrollable belly laughs erupted out of me. It took a minute before I could get words out. "Sure...no problem... we'll just dust it off... It'll be *fine*!... By the way, do you like Indian healing chants? I just bought this album..."

A whole package of Pepperidge Farm cookies later, we'd listened to the entire record and spent hours of exhilarating conversation together. Wrapping up our visit at my apartment door, Michael spontaneously gave me a big 'good-bye' bear hug... which was delightful and absolutely perfect!

Having grown up around D.C. meant that he knew how to get around without getting a parking ticket and also knew of great out-of-the-way places to go and things to do. After that first visit we managed to see each other almost every single day. I'd never had such great company or fantastic conversation or so much fun in my entire life. We also discovered that we shared the same values and had grown up with many of the same challenges as well.

Two weeks later Michael kissed me for the first time. I'd dated quite a bit in college but *THIS* is the stuff movies were made of! Goose bumps and riotous tingling raced up and down throughout my whole body. For the first time *ever,* my toes curled during a kiss! We 'clicked' on all levels! Two months later, on May 24th, we were engaged and married on October 29th. Michael turned out to be the most perfect partner on the planet for me. Until Baba came into my life, Gramma, my little brother and Michael brought me the closest to the energy of God and joy in my world.

# Chapter 3

## Sadhana and My Tool Box

*"Sadhana is essential because the effects of karma have to be removed by karma alone, as a thorn is removed only by another thorn. You cannot remove it by a knife or a hammer or even a sword."*
- Sathya Sai Baba

So, the source of my 'dis-ease' was finally identified as Spiritual Yearning, and I found Baba about five years later, so where do I go from here? My intense, deep homesickness still needed to be wiped out. What did I have to know or do that could uproot it? Could it be replaced with total peace and fullness, even bliss? In hindsight, I think what I was actually after was a way to grasp onto the enormous whole picture that would show me answers and give me a 'reunion' with my spiritual source.

Between all the illuminating conversations with Michael and more research, I finally discovered that this subject has been thoroughly explored for *thousands* of years, with mind-boggling comprehensiveness, especially

41

through Hinduism. Actually, Hinduism takes my limited desire for peace and fulfillment even further and expresses it better than I ever could. Here's one tiny but packed summary: "The quest is for an Ultimate behind which, below which...and beyond which there is nothing. The Ultimate must be that from which *everything* else is derived...free from all limitations of space and time...Brahman." Well...okay, that *more* than covers everything I'm looking for 'behind the curtain'! A great deal regarding Brahman can be found in the Upanishads if you'd like more details. By giving you a sense of the matrix I'm coming from, you'll have a better context for Baba's involvement and impact.

It doesn't come as a surprise that no matter how many things we possess, our 'stuff' can't keep giving us the same degree of happiness; they have an emotional shelf life, even if it's from the fact that over time our joyful excitement from their newness disintegrates. Everything that can change also has some degree of power to control and disappoint and hurt us, which then often triggers a reaction from an egotistical point of view, and that keeps us chained to creating more consequences, karma. Ancient scriptures and Baba teach that to have the greatest, unimaginable joy and wisdom and freedom, the focus needs to turn within, to uncover and merge with the ultimate, which is unchangeable and permanent in life, divine consciousness. If we attain *that,* we have it all! *There's nothing left to want!* Not that we shouldn't enjoy the material things we've acquired in life, but it's important to realize that infinitely more is available beyond that, and it's of greater and permanent value.

An important key is to develop the ability to distinguish between what's real and 'unreal' (or think of it as relatively real). A simple analogy I've heard that makes it pretty clear goes like this: By recognizing that my shadow is not really me (even though it can be seen right next to me), even if ten thousand elephants pass over it, I can still smile and be happy, for I know that no matter how much my shadow is trampled upon, it can't bring *me* any pain.

Once, when I had my store, I mentally asked Baba about the power and esoteric value of the mineral specimens I carried. There's so much written about their influence. Are they important to possess to reach a higher level? His response was quick and concise and in the form of a question. "Why settle for a few stones when you can have the whole mountain?"

The decades' worth of useful spiritual information I've gathered can't be distilled sufficiently to pour into one chapter here but Baba's clear, comprehendible style through His discourses offer a wealth of knowledge and wisdom. After first reading a few books about Him, I began reading about His teachings and found His vahinis, which, for me was a great place to start and worth checking out.

To catch a glimpse of Baba's brilliance (and sometimes humor) in making a point about my spiritual efforts, I've got to let you in on the transformative instruments I've been using for quite some time. They're practical and (mostly) do-able. At first glance, you might consider them quite simplistic, but simple doesn't mean easy; what's important is that they work if I exert enough effort and practice.

Sadhana (pronounced sod, short 'o', den, short 'e', uh, short 'u' as in up) is a spiritual practice used to help purify the heart, mind and body. It scrubs off accumulated (egotistical) dirt and grime, so that inner divinity can be fully revealed. Between having a deep-seated desire to uncover it and doing various sadhanas (in the spirit of worship to God), the chances of success tilt in my favor, big time. Many types of sadhana are available. I tend to think of them as the tools I have to get to the 'pure gold' within. Baba has highlighted some of these tools through His dream visits, particularly in instances where I didn't employ one that would have helped a lot.

Before talking about them, it's been suggested that we think of ourselves as comprised of two parts, the small 'self' and the greater or higher divine 'Self'. The small self is ego-based, acquired attitudes and behavior based on outside influences and conditioning, and contains our vasanas, automatic carry-over tendencies from decisions we've made in the past. It gives me a sense of individuality and separateness from others. It's also where personal selfish desires come from (whether satisfied or thwarted; thwarted desires leading to the 'seven deadly sins'). The higher Self refers to God consciousness, all-knowing, indestructible, eternal, and is not only part of me, but the invisible spirit and substrata of the entire universe. Baba points out what a precious gift it is that humanity has been given the ability to discover its inherent divinity. We uniquely have the ability to learn how to transcend the small self and merge with the perfection of the (God) Self; it's actually considered by hundreds of millions to be the purpose and goal of life on Earth. Steps made toward the higher Self can bring about an exponentially higher quality of life while we're here, too, alive in a physical body.

Baba puts it well:

> "We are not the body, mind, intellect, senses. They are manipulated by us. We are the divine indweller who resides in our spiritual hearts. You have all the powers in you...Do not think that you are human and have to reach the state of the divine. Think rather, that you are God and from

that state have become a human being."

As most of us have already figured out, there are consequences from the choices we make (from the divine gift of free will) and they're both positive and negative and inescapable. They dictate the situations we find ourselves in, given the spiritual growth that still needs to be accomplished. If anyone wonders, karma doesn't require faith; it operates 24/7 over all our lifetimes whether we accept it or not. I think these collective effects of my decisions are what creates my own spiritual blueprint and escorts me into every life. It's a specific plan based on what I've already built (or ignored so far) spiritually. Whether I'm consciously aware of it or not, there is a master plan that shows what still needs to be worked on to bring my individual 'structure' to completion. With few exceptions, we're all under different phases of construction! This tally of all my thoughts and actions is generally known as the akashic record.

Once, Baba was asked if He is God here on Earth. His response was, "I am God and you, too are God. The only difference between you and me is that while I am aware of it, you are completely unaware."

Ralph Waldo Emerson also embraced the ancient eastern concept that divinity is inherent in all of humanity. He went on to postulate that we can be spiritual without being religious, and I don't disagree, but sometimes the structure of religion can be comforting. Hinduism offers more than a religion; it's a philosophy and culture too, emotionally ringing true to me and fills in the blanks more than any other religion I've come across.

What a difference a change in perspective can make in attitude! The Catholic religion of my childhood served only to instill fear, guilt, obligation and submission to its self-serving rules. In its doctrine I was and would always be a sinner. Period. That's the baseline and there was no choice but to proceed from there.

Regardless of our backgrounds and attitudes, reality seems to be based on only two factors, our vantage point and our karma. Remember several decades ago when stereoscopic art became popular? When you first looked at the picture all you could see was a zig-zaggy colorful blob. It wasn't possible to see the 'real' picture if you looked at it in the usual way. Luckily, instructions were available. By first holding the picture up to your nose, relaxing your eyes, and slowly moving it away from your face, voila! A perfectly clear 3-D picture emerged. It took information and effort to go through the necessary process, though, to see the real picture. I admit, this example is an understatement in terms of spiritual growth, but you will see in upcoming pages Baba's readiness and ability to show how to bring the real picture into focus. It will also become clear that it's only a tiny fraction of all He's willing to give to those who want Him in their life and are willing to trust and rely on Him. From decades of experience, I'm convinced that the only gratitude Baba looks for is my spiritual growth and transformation, adding greater divine light to humanity.

According to Him and other scriptures, the purification of negative thoughts and emotions, like hatred and anger, provides a way to release the delusions we hold on to, and is vital in removing the agitations and misery in life. Above everything else, developing greater love is essential and is the goal of undertaking sadhana.

There's one particular perspective that can be helpful if taken into account, and it seems to pop up all over on many intellectual levels, whether you hear it from Baba or are truckin' through Shankara's Vivekachudamani or simply listening to the lyrics of an American children's song. "Row, row, row your boat gently down the stream. Merrily, merrily, merrily, merrily; *life is but a dream.*" It's so simple but so full of symbology. The boat is my body, the vehicle that encompasses my divine essence, which carries me down the stream (along the journey of life on Earth). Merrily (said four times!) reinforces that I should be very happy about it! "Life is but a dream" is the reason why! It implores us to take the life experience lightly and not get bogged down because it's only *relatively* real, a dream. No matter how dramatic or vivid the scenario as we sleep at night, when we wake up in the morning all dreams dissipate into nothingness. So too, with this Earthly reality. Although we have to fully participate in life (since we agreed to come here for a reason), and work on completing the blueprint, we can choose not to be embroiled in it all.

My take-away from abundant literature on the subject is that the nature of the world, our spiritual classroom, is duality, the apparent differences and opposites that create conflict in life. Our interactions and choices by living here is the medium we have for spiritual growth, to take ourselves beyond the duality and back to the underlying Oneness, the real and whole picture of who we are. Developing greater purity in thoughts and actions brings me to the interim goal, great karma. Ultimately, though, when I get to the point where unselfish, pure love is the only motivator of all my thoughts and actions, there is no karma at all and no need for spiritual growth or the struggles of another human birth. This total freedom from delusion is called liberation or moksha and achieving it cuts the tight, heart-wrenching bonds created through attachments while we're here in the birth, death, rebirth cycle.

Another tip is to learn how to work effectively and, among other things, how to steady the mind. Like a person who wants the exceptionally high physical achievement of winning a full Ironman triathlon, efficient, sustained training and committed discipline are also mandatory, not optional, for spiritual attainment. A work-out routine must be set up based on strengths and weaknesses. No matter how much raw talent a person has, improvement will be necessary. No one becomes a world class athlete, no matter how much he or she wants it, spending all day being a couch potato!

The spiritual 'muscle groups' to work with, the pillars of Baba's teachings, include **Truth** (finding it and aligning thought word and deed to it, known as sathya), **Righteousness** (conduct that fulfills our moral and ethical duty, called dharma), **Unconditional Love**, (unselfishly motivated, prema), **Peace** (unshakable mental and emotional equilibrium under all circumstances, called shanti), and **Non-violence** (in both actions and thoughts, also known as ahimsa).

Briefly, the Bhagavad Gita talks about three stages on the spiritual path. To sum it up in one sentence, we have to know God is here, we have to have a distinct vision of God, and then we have to merge with God. That's it. Could I figure out everything I'd have to do to accomplish this by myself? Not likely; maybe not impossible, but definitely not likely. The results from my efforts are much more productive with the expertise and support of 'Someone' who really knows what I need to work on and has already successfully 'coached' other elite athletes.

Baba offers more than spiritual wisdom. His compassion, miracles, leelas, boons and humor help me keep my head in the game even when I stumble and doubt my ability and don't live up to my own expectations. As others have said through different analogies, no matter how long it takes to find the best 'coach', once the decision is made it's important to commit and trust His or Her judgment, even if dramatic results aren't immediate. If I'm digging underground for water and want to hit a huge aquifer so I have access to a life-long well, it would be awfully costly and disappointing if I only go down a foot in dozens of different places. It's important to choose the right one and go deep!

Practical exercises begin right after getting a handle on the qualities of the nature of things and people so I can develop more control in helping my Self emerge. The Bhagavad Gita refers to these qualities as gunas and there are three of them, each highly influential. By understanding how they affect me, I can minimize unwanted influences and increase the kind of energy that will be helpful. There's a lot on the subject if you want to Google it, but I'm going to present it in a nutshell, enough to give the gist of each of them.

The first is satwic energy. It's pure, calm, clear and balanced; spiritually the highest. Emotionally it's connected to equanimity, selfless love and compassion. Next, there's the rajasic element. It's passionate, active, and agitated, sometimes chaotic. Emotionally it's connected to restlessness, irritation and anger. Then there's tamasic energy. It's dull, lethargic and dark. It's associated with laziness, depression and ignorance. In any given moment we tend to be exposed to a combination of all three to some extent, but the weight of what we allow in or choose *not* to allow in can be deliberately altered.

If I take in more satwic energy and the rajasic and tamasic are reduced, substantial spiritual progress can be made. The vibration of everything affects thoughts and feelings and even the body to a degree. So what does this actually mean? I need to pay close attention and notice everything I'm taking in and make smarter choices. For instance, let's start with food. On a spiritual path, satwic food is the most beneficial because it's naturally of a higher vibration as well as nutrient rich. It's vegetarian and includes most locally grown organic fresh fruits and vegetables, dairy products, nuts and seeds, organic whole grains, legumes and unrefined sugars. Rajasic foods tend to excite and invigorate; its agitating energy includes things that are spicy hot, bitter, sour or pungent. Tamasic foods have the lowest vibrational energy and are generally harmful on many fronts. They include meat, fish and fowl, which, among other things, often contain unwanted antibiotics or toxins from polluted waters. Also in this category are refined processed foods, including white, bleached flour and all kinds of sweets, probably doused with pesticides and filled with chemicals you can't pronounce, including artificial colors, flavors, preservatives, stabilizers, and refined sugar. They are more likely to be genetically modified too. This dead food can't give a person the sustenance he or she needs on any level. So, bottom line, by taking a look at where my 'ratios' are and adjusting them in favor of satwic energy, my purification process is already underway!

Besides the food I take in, I also need to monitor what comes out of my mouth. Speech can be very highly charged energetically and sometimes I think the words I use have a greater impact on me than the person I'm directing them to. Baba talks about the need to learn to restrain the tongue. Before speaking, He recommends asking ourselves, "Does what I have to say improve upon the silence?" Another suggestion of His on the topic is that even if you can't oblige another person, you can always speak obligingly. Good advice, nothing I would have thought of myself. Have to admit, this recommendation isn't exactly a walk in the park for an Italian Leo...

There are two corollaries of speech that can also be used to increase satwic energy. The first is devotional singing. This includes doing bhajans, singing hymns or other inspirational music and chanting sacred mantras and prayers. A quick aside here, there's a perfect little Vedic prayer (Asato ma...) that beautifully and concisely petitions for truth and transcendence: From the unreal (duality) lead me to the real (Oneness, Brahman), from darkness (ignorance) lead me to light (truth), from mortality (death, part of the inevitable cycle in the realm of duality) lead me to immortality (freedom from it through divine consciousness).

Conversely to what can be expressed, it's also helpful *not* to listen to or look at low vibrational input. These would be words and sounds that are harsh and discordant or can give nightmares, whether it's heavy metal or a horror flick or the evening news. They all tend to be tremendously rajasic and/or tamasic. By watching the news much less often than I used to, I haven't missed out on anything good! I feel a little lighter, to be honest. Actually, everything we read or watch or listen to for entertainment ought to be evaluated in terms of its gunas.

Although a good balance can be struck, for the sake of a boost from a spiritual standpoint, the more satwic, the better! In the same vein, people we choose to spend time with on a regular basis should be taken a look at through the lens of the gunas, too. Identify their predominant energy. Do they always tend to be in or on the verge of an emotional crisis or upset or angry about something (rajasic)? Are they often depressed and stuck in a rut and only complain rather than do anything about it (tamasic)? Or is their presence peaceful and calming, like a breath of fresh air, and automatically makes you feel better (satwic)?

Although some days are better than others, I do make an effort for my Self to bring in more satwic energy. It can make a big difference in dealing with those pesky spiritual growth opportunities that keep cropping up. I've noticed they don't go away if I don't deal with them, just sprout up in a different place and time. By approaching them from higher ground, I have an advantage. Also, an added feature, by being more satwic (unselfishly loving and compassionate), it may 'rub off' on those around us...certainly only a good thing!

Another tool, not as common in our culture as in the East, is repeating the name you're comfortable with of your favorite form of God, known as namasmarana. It can produce immediate and effective results, any time of the day, anywhere. The name alone, said from the heart with fervor, can actually invoke the presence and power of God. It not only purifies the energy in your space, it can give protection from physical harm. Baba has exemplified this in more than one dream for me (see the More Baba Dream Visits chapter).

The last few suggestions in connection with speech, actually the lack thereof, are the practices of meditation, silence and breath control. They're widely known and accepted and, at the very least, can reduce rajasic energy. With proper practice they can also lead to a connection to the higher Self.

A final 'tool' I'll share here is the most heavy-duty of them all. It's selfless service to others, widely known as seva (the 'e' is pronounced as a long 'a' as in they). Although most are familiar with the concept of volunteering to do service, doing seva requires us to also check our ego at the door. It's purely motivated and can be thought of as love and compassion in action, totally satwic. Baba gives specific guidelines on it:

> "Do not serve for the sake of reward, attracting attention, or earning gratitude, or from a sense of pride at your own superiority in skill, wealth, status or authority. Serve because you are urged by

Love. When you succeed, ascribe the success to the Grace of God, who urged you on as Love within you."

One last item deserving of mention is not a tool but a key element in setting the pace of spiritual progress. It is the mindset of 'surrender'. I totally understand anyone out there who's suddenly raising an eyebrow suspiciously. The generally accepted definition goes totally against my grain, too. For decades I didn't fully grasp what it meant as it relates to spiritual growth or see its value, and it also sounded a little scary, so I ignored it. To most of us, surrender implies losing and giving up personal control and freedom, and submitting to the will of someone else, the winner. Why would I ever willingly do that? Wouldn't my life go flying out of control if I surrendered? Who would take care of fulfilling my desires better than I and who would I surrender to and how would that look in terms of day-to-day life?

My attitude was based on two incorrect premises. First was the idea that whatever I'd be surrendering is of value, and second, that it's taken from me by someone else who is forcing me to submit. It's taken much longer than I'd like to admit to realize the truth, but I feel I finally have. Spiritual surrender is only the willingness to relinquish the gratification of non-beneficial petty desires for my 'self', (not of real value or permanent and possibly harmful) for the realization of my 'Self', which will provide ultimate fulfillment and permanent joy and a better, healthier life while I'm here. So I'm only submitting and surrendering my 'self' to my 'Self'! It's a win-win!

# Chapter 4

## High Five!

*"Where a person is fully surrendered to God, Baba acts in the mode of Divine Mother, caring for and guarding that devotee, doing more for the devotee than the devotee could ever imagine to ask for."*
- Sathya Sai Baba

When it comes to spiritual growth, it's been surprising to discover it's when I'm *not* thinking about it and least expect it that I make the most progress. Understanding spiritual information is a dynamic mental process for me that involves analysis and discernment, but absorbing spiritual truth has been a quiet, subtle process over time that has nothing to do with thinking. It seems to seep in gently and slowly and then sets rock-solid. The transformation it brings about could be huge but it's not glaring. Often I don't notice it at all until I see it in hindsight. Baba, however, notices my spiritual mile-markers immediately whether I do or not, and occasionally acknowledges it with a 'High Five!' like no other! Here's one stunning example.

In 1981, for Christmas Michael gave me a 14 karat gold ring that held a small deep purple amethyst gemstone in it. I didn't have any other amethyst jewelry and it cost him more than he should have spent or could really afford at the time. I cherished it and wore it every day.

A few months later, in the spring, I took a trip for the weekend to visit friends, Linda and Bill, a married couple and Sai Baba devotees. They'd recently returned from Baba's ashram in India and I was looking forward to hearing all about it. As I wound around the mountains of Pennsylvania on route 15, my amethyst ring sat securely on my right ring finger as it always did. I remember wiggling it slightly with my thumb now and then while driving just to admire the deep purple sparkle as it caught the sun.

The three of us had a great weekend and I left feeling as though I'd had Baba's darshan, too. However, on the way home my contentment was overshadowed by sheer panic when I saw that my amethyst ring was no longer on my finger. I hadn't taken it off and it wasn't too large, so it couldn't have slid off. The minute I got home I unpacked and carefully checked everything in the suitcase, including all the pockets of the clothes I'd brought with me. I even picked up the empty suitcase and shook it vigorously upside down. Nothing. I also emptied my toiletry bag, a place I never would have put jewelry to begin with. I checked the seats and floor of the car too. It wasn't anywhere. This was nuts...and so irritating! In frustration and out of places to look, I called Linda to ask her to check around her house for it. She couldn't find it either. I don't know how, when, or where it happened, but my amethyst ring seemed to have vanished. *Dammit!* Over the next several weeks I rechecked everything at least a dozen times that I'd brought on the trip before finally giving up the search. I honestly didn't think it was my fault (because I didn't take it off!) but still couldn't help feeling guilty and disappointed in myself for having lost that special Christmas gift from Michael. Fortunately, this isn't the end of the story.

Four years later, in 1985, Rebecca, our youngest child who was two at the time, needed to go back to Georgetown University Hospital for a third surgery, this one unplanned. It was the third of thirteen major surgeries she'd undergo by the age of twelve. I'd had a miscarriage of her twin eight weeks into my pregnancy and it affected the development of openings in her body. Among other issues, she was born with a complete bilateral cleft lip and palate. Her tiny lip was repaired (with *fifty-two* sutures) when she was just two months old. A year later a soft palate (the roof to her mouth) was created but a few months after that operation it developed a tear and needed to be fixed right away.

Michael and I both took Rebecca to the hospital and we did the Gayatri mantra together en route (Baba has said to *never* give up the Gayatri). The whole family can feel the protection and comfort in it and we all start and end the day with it, whether we're all under the same roof or not. After finishing the prayer, I made it my mission to make lots of little rainbows just for Rebecca. If the sun was out and I could catch it just right in my diamond, dozens of little round 'rainbow' light refractions would dance all over inside the car. Being surrounded by dancing rainbows seemed to be the only thing guaranteed to bring a smile to her face on operation day.

We waited together until the procedure was over and Rebecca was brought up to her room. Then I stayed with her in Pediatric Intensive Care the entire time, while Michael went home to hold down the fort for our other children, six and four at that time.

In an attempt to emotionally reconcile it, I tried analyzing the whole situation from a logical point of view. I'm not a smoker or a drinker and I don't do drugs. I'm a good cook, know a lot about nutrition and, for the most part, eat well all the time, not just during pregnancies. I wasn't under a lot of stress and didn't work outside our home until all the children were in school full-time. Michael helped me a lot around the house; there was no undue physical exertion. He took care of everything from doing dishes and laundry, to wrapping me in his arms with more than usual wonderful bear hugs. I couldn't think of a single thing I could have changed to prevent the way Rebecca was born, and neither can I put into words how horribly sorry I felt for her. She exuded such an angelic, calm, delicate energy. How much physical pain would she go through because of this? How much would she suffer emotionally as a child and teenager? Thinking about the 'what ifs' was devastating.

Adding to this stress stood my life-long fear of hospitals. From the first time I remember entering one, my body has always reacted with a 'fight-or-flight' response... rapid shallow breathing, a pounding heart, sweaty palms and nausea. Luckily, I've rarely needed to be in one for myself but the reaction is there even when I'm just visiting! Rebecca was going through so much; I was determined to cover up this anxiety for her sake. The only time I let my guard down was at night when she slept.

I hope none of you are familiar with the experience of living with your child in Pediatric Intensive Care. Taking care of everything that needed to be repaired was going to be a lengthy process over a period of years, but I knew that Rebecca's problems were fixable. Some children on that floor were unlikely to be released alive. We were lucky to have the best, the chief of reconstructive surgery, but when I saw her face bruised and swollen almost beyond recognition, laying limp from anesthesia and pain meds, the high metal guardrails up on both sides of her bed and an IV needle stuck in her and all the wires from monitors attached to her fragile little two year old body...

Georgetown is a teaching hospital so in addition to the doctor and nurse (and a couple of geneticists), different interns traipsed in and out at all hours of the day and night, too, taking a peek, asking the same questions and interrupting my ragged sleep on the 'sleep-chair' next to Rebecca's bed. Days dragged on like months but I helped her feel safe and proud that she was doing such a good job and I let her know (often) that her surgery was a big success.

Although she improved every day, my stress levels didn't change a lot. The more she began to heal, the more restless she became. She wanted the IV out. She wanted to be with her Daddy and brother and sister. She didn't want the food she needed. I had to deal with it. The only respite was when Michael came to visit with the children. Their cheerful visits made everything seem better but still, I couldn't wait to get home and get life back to normal and sleep in our own beds.

With past surgeries we could go home after being released from Pediatric Intensive Care. We never had to stay in the hospital more than a week. This time the doctor ordered to have Rebecca transferred to the regular children's floor after seven days. He wanted to keep an eye on her longer due to a small infection in one of the sutures in her mouth.

After ten days of it, the stress, the sleep deprivation, and being hemmed in by hospital walls and well-meaning strangers, I hit my wall. I'm not proud of my attitude but enough was enough! I couldn't take anymore! Rebecca's swelling had subsided considerably and the dark purple bruising on her face had faded to yellowish green. I knew I could keep a close watch on her at home. I saw how the sutures needed to be cleaned with the swab and hydrogen peroxide. We'd already been through two other surgeries and I knew the protocol of feeding her.

As much as Rebecca was antsy to go home, I wanted to go home even more. I decided to take matters into my own hands. We *had* to get released! When her doctor came in that day, I had my practiced little speech ready and delivered it flawlessly. His reply was simple, unflinching and to the point, "No. It would be better for her to stay a little longer." The response felt like a denial for parole. Seconds after that blow of rejection I started fuming inside and knew that *I* was going to make that decision. It took just an instant to mentally weigh the options. I could take control, argue my point, even leave without permission if necessary, or... relinquish my desires and needs and acquiesce to what the doctor felt was best. From an emotional standpoint I was totally drawn to the first option but unexpectedly, something stronger inside me pushed its way to the forefront. I missed my family and the comforts of home enormously and honestly didn't think we still needed to be in the hospital, but somehow I kept my mouth shut and disheartedly sided with the doctor, with a slight nod as I looked away from him.

Getting ready for bed that night, or, more accurately, getting ready for 'chair', I went into the bathroom to dig out my toothbrush and toothpaste from the toiletry bag. Unzipping it and lifting the cover as I had every day in the hospital, this time my body and brain seemed to freeze for a second as it tried to absorb what I was seeing. Then an involuntary, noisy gasp escaped, causing Rebecca to stir in her sleep. *OH MY GOD!* YES, there it was, my 'lost' amethyst ring! Sitting in the center of my make-up bag, right on *top*, on top of the toothpaste, deodorant and everything, was my amethyst Christmas ring! My heart pounded uncontrollably as I snatched it up and tears spilled over. It was *absolutely impossible* for that ring to be sitting there, but there it was! For several minutes I couldn't do anything except stand there and stare at it in my hand and sob out loud. *Oh, BABA! THANK YOU! THANK YOU!!!* He knew *everything* I'd been going through and saw that brief moment of surrender in my decision to relinquish my will and desires, and He gave me a tangible 'High Five' of congratulations!

I'd read about Baba's omniscience and spontaneous manifestations for years but hadn't ever expected to witness it in person. As thrilled as I was to have my ring from Michael returned, I was even more elated to have had this dramatic first-hand experience showing how Baba is here with me and for me. He replaced my stress and discomfort with overwhelming joy and gratitude, all in an instant! I'm happy to report that since its re-appearance, I've been able to hold on to Michael's gift, thirty-six years and counting!

Baba has addressed the topic of surrender on many occasions through His dream visits. I've recounted a few of them here: Baba dream – August, 1992

Preface: In the past three years I've been to India twice and noticed a deep-seated affinity and familiarity there. When I see needy children there, it somehow hurts me more and my motherly instincts rev into high gear. Ideally, I'd bring them all home with me to make sure they're given everything they need.

In this dream I found myself at the edge of some huge, parade-type event. Thousands of people were involved. Baba was in charge and, at times, would assume different physical forms. Amid the blazing heat of the day, this enormous procession was fully underway. I was the only American there and was observing everything from the sidelines. It seemed that everybody was totally absorbed, doing their small part almost furtively to keep up. Baba was leading the whole thing, directing and orchestrating, setting the path and pace of movement. I even saw Him cutting down some brush that was in the way. Pujas (prescribed ceremonies from ancient scriptures) were also going on in the midst of it. At one point Baba transformed into a thin, old woman and commanded that the food be brought. Immediately a glass of milk (unpasteurized and fresh from the cow!) was handed to Her. She looked directly at me in exasperation, "I ask for food and they bring wine!" I didn't understand this comment because I didn't see any wine (a hint, maybe, that our perspectives weren't the same?).

Several tables were set up. As Baba (in the feminine form) walked by, lots of different items instantaneously appeared on them. I noticed a lace tablecloth on one table and an elderly woman was carefully pouring milk from a pitcher directly on to the table. Why would she do that? The milk ran in a little rivulet across the table and was about to spill over the edge. I couldn't help bringing it to her attention by blurting out. She calmly noticed but instead of rushing to get a cloth to wipe it up, she casually carried over a pitcher for the liquid to pour into as it spilled; not exactly what I would have done.

Although the whole enormous procession bordered on chaotic, men, women and children were doing their little parts even if it wasn't always quite right according to my way of thinking. They were all involved in something greater than themselves, something good and productive and it was (literally) moving forward with tremendous momentum, and Baba was leading the way.

I saw that there wasn't a role for me. Apparently, I didn't always have Baba's perspective and couldn't even understand why some things were done at all. I realized that I had to release the attachment to my desire to be personally involved in helping destitute children in India. It seemed that Baba not only wanted me to see this but to know that it's okay; He has it all under control.

Baba dream - September, 1994 - I was with a long-time, wonderful friend, ShivaKumar. We were going to a special puja that Baba was going to personally conduct. I hadn't been to anything like it before (I don't know if there even is such a puja in normal waking life), but I knew Kumar was familiar with it. Surprisingly, there were very few people in attendance, even though there was capacity for several hundred. Without seeing the source, I heard a voice inform me, "More people will be coming... later."

Here, protocol dictated that when Baba passed in front of each person he or she would offer (surrender) something of his or her choice. It could range from very small to enormously significant. It was a total free-will offering to God decided upon by the donor. I saw a six-year old student give some school supplies. I also noticed a large bin filled with donated paper clips. It looked like a lot of people had given very little.

Baba emerged. Kumar and I were in awe of His magnificent presence and proximity. Even more breathtaking was the intensity of love emanating from Him. When He stopped in front of us, He looked directly at me and nodded encouragingly, giving permission to give what I wanted to give Him. I handed over a small piece of paper describing what I would give for divinity. Kumar did the same. Baba accepted our pledges and continued on. A few minutes later He came around to each of us a second time. Kumar was prepared and ready to give Baba another offering. I couldn't believe he was giving even more; I knew he'd given a lot the first time. I wasn't aware that I should have been prepared to give more right away. It suddenly dawned on me that it was the reason so few people were in the room. Offering up our 'stuff', (whether material or egotistical traits) tends to occur mainly when people think their lives are close to an end. What most don't see is that when we hand over our attachments for God's sake, we're uncovering more of our own divine nature. The result is a much higher net gain, not a loss. The more selfish ties we sever (renounce), the freer (more liberated) we become of everything that binds us to Earth. Baba has explained this subject thoroughly but I like His brief, bottom-line advice: "Less baggage, more comfort!"

Baba dream - April, 1998 - There was a tremendous amount going on; lots of people, interactions and involvements. I was aware of it but separated from it by a dozen yards or so, observing rather than being in the midst of it all. Then I noticed a big, black frame surrounding it, giving the impression that it was all happening inside an enormous television and wasn't even real .

Baba suddenly appeared next to me, standing so close that our shoulders touched. His 'best-friend' familiar vibration was welcomed. He looked happy and satisfied that we were watching all the stuff going on together from a distance. The simple impression I was left with was that it's good to take a few steps back, to detach and not get embroiled in all the drama of the everyday stuff. This idea's been around for a long time but I guess I needed a reminder.

# Chapter 5

## Bernice and the Baba Boon

*"Give all your burdens to God. Be light and free. Have sacred faith. Without faith there is no success in life."*
- Sathya Sai Baba

Remember the early '90s when interest rates skyrocketed and the country took a nose dive into a recession? I'll never forget it. I sat in my shop in historic downtown Frederick, Maryland with little else to do but listen to the deafening silence of my dying business. Like most downtown retailers, I wasn't selling anything people needed, just wanted. I carried gemstone jewelry and semi-precious beaded strands, as well as individual beads so customers could design and make their own jewelry, too. There were also gift items – chimes, contemporary glass oil lamps, quartz 'singing' bowls and Swarovski studded greeting cards. What I enjoyed acquiring most for the store, though, were the striking, one-of-a-kind mineral carvings. Among hundreds of unique pieces at

Sunburst Treasures, we were the only place around where you could buy a Coober Pedy fire opal carved rabbit or a sugilite elephant or even an exquisitely sculpted malachite Buddha from Zaire. Once I even bought and sold a life-sized labradorite owl for a customer, just stunning. It was always exciting to attend the annual world-wide lapidary show in Tucson, where I found many of these treasures. But, again, what I carried were things people wanted, not what they needed. With disposable income drying up fast for so many, Michael and I had to cancel the Tucson trip that year.

With few exceptions, my regular customers became irregular and almost half dropped off altogether. As our daily sales continued to plummet I stopped taking a salary. It got to the point where there was almost nothing left after covering overhead. Then our finances turned much worse.

After the summer season was over at Wild World, the D.C. area's only water-theme amusement park, the owners decided to sell, and along with other top management, Michael's position as Park Services Director came to an end. In less than a blink our family income was drastically slashed. As a family of five, our savings dwindled fast and within months disappeared. Credit card bills couldn't be paid. Gymnastic classes and ballet lessons had to stop. It became necessary to sell our home, and we found a house to rent, amazingly still in Middletown. We made ends meet living mostly on the profit from the sale of our house.

Italians have a word that doesn't fully translate into English – aah-ji-da, (accent on the 'aah'). Having many subtle nuances, this word encompasses a sensation of churning, stomach-curdling stress along with a touch of anger and desire to lash out in revenge on whomever or whatever caused it. I tried meditating to calm down and re-center but my aahjida got the best of me.

There were no other major amusement parks in the area and since we didn't want to uproot our family to another part of the country, Michael had to change professions. He'd been in charge of day-to-day operations at Wild World, which was a position with many facets, including the supervision of more than three hundred summertime personnel. It over-qualified him for dozens of possibilities locally. It took almost two years before he transitioned to another field and things got back on track financially. However, at that point we didn't have two extra pennies for a down payment on a house. So when the owners of the house we were renting informed us that they were putting the house on the market, we knew we'd have to move again.

It sold much faster than we'd hoped. I tried not to panic but we were down to less than a month before we had to be out, and still had no idea where we were going. Our Middletown schools had all earned the Presidential Blue Ribbon Award of Excellence and our children were happy and doing well there. We'd established roots in Middletown but rental houses were next to impossible to find and we were already in one! Our families couldn't do much. They weren't close; mine were in Auburn, New York, six hours away, and Michael's in Cocoa Beach, Florida, even further.

From spiritual principles I'd learned through Baba, I knew that if I could just set aside my aahjida and fears and detach emotionally from the whole situation, I could get insight and help. I went back to the meditation room, more determined than ever to get centered. Exerting all the concentration I could muster, I shut my eyes, took three very deep cleansing breaths, chanted three aums and did three Gayatri Mantras.

In my mind's eye I saw the whole predicament manifest into this ball of kinetic energy, tiny agitated squiggles of light. Mentally I pushed it out of my head and saw it hover in front of me. Physically I backed away from it. Although it only lasted a couple of minutes, I did feel myself emotionally surrender and give it all up to God to deal with. Calmness replaced my agitation. I saw Baba standing in front of me, beaming with such joy. My heart connected to

His and He smiled at me. Just brimming with love and compassion, His radiance was a soothing balm beyond description. However, I refused to let myself dwell in the moment for long. I was there for answers! Ignoring the fact that He is omniscient, I explained our situation in detail before asking where we should search for a rental house. Pen in hand, I was ready to write down the name of a street or at least the part of Frederick County we should be looking in. He didn't say anything, so I waited. He continued to smile at me and under normal circumstances it would have been reassuring, but I was just confused. *What is this? Didn't He hear me? He knows I need information... details! Time's running out!* Still nothing. Becoming more impatient by the minute, I couldn't believe Baba was right there with me but not saying a word. I held on a little longer but then retreated from the meditation room in a huff, exasperated and irritated, and I went to find Michael to vent to. When I told him what happened, he looked at me and shook his head, almost imperceptibly, trying hard not to show his obvious amusement. "Karen, Baba *smiled* at you... so don't worry!" Right... so much for surrender.

The next afternoon I got a call from Bernice, a regular customer of mine whose husband had died just two weeks before. The mineral carvings were her only interest in my store and she had an insatiable curiosity about them. I could never make a simple sale with Bernice. When she was interested in a rhodochrosite egg, she had to know why there were jagged, cream colored patterns in it. Her never-ending questions regularly forced me to do research. With the innocence and curiosity of a child who wants to know why the sky is blue, Bernice had to know why sugilite is purple. I didn't mind though and actually enjoyed the creative challenge of finding her answers. Our mutual appreciation of the incredible beauty formed by nature created a special bond between us.

One thing that always worried me about her, though, was that based on her outward appearance, it didn't look like she could afford the pieces she bought. She always dressed in a simple cotton housedress and showed no signs of personal indulgence. She cut her own hair, which was sadly evident, and always paid in cash. I worried whether she should be spending what little money she had on carvings. Michael told me not to judge.

Anyway, back to Bernice's phone call. She had an urgent-sounding, rather mysterious request. She asked me to come to her house immediately to help her do something, but I wasn't to tell anyone where I was going. I'd never been invited over before and she'd never asked me to help her with anything except for purchases in the store. I'd only been to her home once, to give my condolences and drop off a food platter after her husband died. I knew she had no children or close siblings and, since Michael was in the store when she called, I told her, "Okay, I can be there in fifteen minutes." I didn't tell Michael anything except that I needed to run out for a little bit.

Pulling into the long gravel driveway of Bernice's tiny brick rancher, I found her peeking suspiciously out through the little half curtain at the kitchen door. A petite woman in her mid-60's, she had straight, brown hair in a style oddly reminiscent of Buster Brown. Not exactly a threatening sight, yet somehow I felt like I should have a password. I didn't need to knock. She unlocked the door and stepped back about a foot, barely allowing enough room for me to slip through. I wondered if I'd been followed. If I had, it was for damn sure no one else was getting in behind me. Something was wrong. You could see it in her face.

"Hi!" I said brightly, attempting a façade of normalcy.

She passed on the social graces. In a voice tinged with disgust she told me, "Come and look at this!" There in the middle of the kitchen table sat a large pile of cash at least three feet in diameter and more than two feet tall. I just stared at it, confused. "The bastard!" she exploded. "I was clearing out the closet in Charlie's bedroom and on the top shelf, all the way over, I found a box with this in it. Can you believe it? Forty-six years of marriage and the rotten bastard never took me on a single vacation! He always made me think there was no extra money." Then, without skipping a beat her attitude shifted, "Would you help me count it?"

This surreal request forced me to squash (swallow, actually) my sudden urge to burst out laughing (which would have been totally inappropriate). With the most serious, straight face I could present, I told her, "Sure, I can help you count it." You know, I'd never been asked to help count a mountain of money before. It was strange, but the more we sorted and counted, the more we relaxed into it and the more fun it became, like playing with Monopoly money, only better. Eventually the mountain turned into tall, neatly stacked rows covering the entire kitchen table. There were no small bills. I told her my total. She shook her head, glaring at the money with contempt. Abruptly, without a word, Bernice got up from the table, crossed over to the broom closet and brought back a paper grocery bag. Shaking it open, she dumped a few stacks in and shoved it into my arms. "Here. You take this. I'm sure you can use it. Now close up the bag good so nothing flies out accidentally."

There was enough money in the bag for a down payment on a house! I'm not often at a loss for words but I think I went into shock; I couldn't say a word! My gratitude could only be seen by the spontaneous flow of tears running non-stop down my face. Bernice wasn't one for sentimentality. She gave me a quick wink. "I know. Yes, well, you're welcome. Now you'd better get going."

She led the way, all twelve feet or so, back to the kitchen door, stood very close to it as she had before, and carefully unlocked the deadbolt to let me out. With both arms wrapped around my grocery bag, it was a monumental effort to walk back to the car; my whole body was trembling. I could feel her eyes on me and glanced back at the house to see her peeking out to watch me go. This time, there was an almost elfish little grin on her face.

Before starting the car I took several deep, slow breaths with especially long exhales so I wouldn't pass out while driving. When I returned it was past closing time but Michael was waiting patiently although wondering what I was up to. I locked us in, turned off the overhead lights and handed him my tightly clutched paper bag. "Look!" As he did, his eyes widened and eyebrows lifted. With deliberate calmness in his voice, he looked up from the bag to make direct eye contact with me. Ever so gently, he asked me, "Karen... *where have you been?*"

Never could I have imagined a more unlikely scenario for solving our financial dilemma. Talk about God working in mysterious ways! The light bulb suddenly went on as to why Baba was *so* happy when we were together in the meditation room. He knew! He had this all planned and He'd orchestrated the whole thing! What a leela! As astounding as this is, there's even more to this Baba boon.

First, though, for those who are curious, here's a little follow-up on Bernice. A couple of weeks later she and her dead husband's lawyer were going through Charlie's office together at the bottling plant and discovered two savings bank books tucked away in the back of his desk drawer. They totaled just over 1.6 million dollars... She called me again with an even more unusual request, wanting me to contact the cemetery where Charlie was buried. She needed to find out if after the headstone is in the ground did it still belong to her or was it the cemetery's property? If it was hers, she'd decided that *we* were going for a drive along with her sledgehammer to pay Charlie a visit at Mount St. Olivet's. She said that nothing in life could give her greater satisfaction than smashing Charlie's headstone to smithereens. I was enormously relieved to find out that once installed, a headstone *does* automatically become the property of the cemetery. Fuming, Bernice shared her not-so-subtle feelings, "I'd give anything to have Charlie back for five more minutes...just so I could kill him myself!"

Now, with cash in hand for a down payment on a house and just under a month to vacate the rental, we investigated all possibilities in our price range. Many of them were beyond Middletown's school district. As much as keeping our children in Middletown was our desire and a priority, having a roof over our heads in three weeks was a higher one. We scoured newspapers and Michael checked the internet. We did drive-bys and set up appointments all over Frederick County. None of the houses were right. Still, after what Baba had just manifested for us to be able to buy a house, I had no doubt that somehow something would work out. We kept looking.

Less than a week after being given the money I was in our car pulling out of the driveway when a husband and wife out for a walk in the neighborhood strolled into our cul-de-sac. The man noticed some dead branches that Michael had cut and stacked by the road from a recent heavy storm. I noticed the little wagon he was pulling and obliged when he asked if he could have the stack for their wood-burning stove. As he loaded the wood, his eyes wandered to the For Sale sign still on the front lawn. Conversationally he mentioned that he had just put his house on the market, too, just two days ago, and was selling it himself. The advertisement in the paper hadn't even come out yet. I explained that we weren't the owners of the house and were actually in the market to buy. Without a second's hesitation, he asked me if I'd like to buy his house. It was located on Willowtree Drive, *the very next street over!* My heart pounded as I bombarded him with questions and found myself nodding repeatedly, hearing answers I liked. Michael and I went to see the house the same day. It had the location, number of bedrooms and fireplace we wanted, as well as an unexpected large, glass-enclosed sunroom off the kitchen, which opened to a big back yard and then a farmer's cornfield and then a spectacular, unobstructed mountain view. It looked like the house came with hundreds of private acres instead of the half acre it actually sat on. This brick rancher was built in the seventies and needed an updated kitchen but it was perfect for our needs, in our price range, *and* our children wouldn't need to change schools! It took less than sixty seconds of private consultation in their sunroom for us to come to a unanimous decision; we made a full-price offer on the spot. It was accepted and we were able to move in within the month. The house became our home for fourteen years, until after Michael's passing in 2008. We replaced the kitchen and Michael finished off the walk-out basement. When I sold it I received *two and a half times* what we paid for it.

Between this experience and hundreds of others since first seeing His picture in 1981, Baba's proven to me that He is *always* there for me, no matter what. His love and protection have never wavered and because of Him I have much more strength than I'd have otherwise to get through things. As I've said, thanking Him is best expressed by continuing to make the effort to attain what He and I both want for me, to become a brighter embodiment of love, for my own sake and joy, and for the upliftment of others. The energy of humanity could be so much higher and happier.

I know I've made this point before, but I'm reiterating - whether Baba is in a physical body on Earth now or not has *no bearing* on His availability or power to help any of us on a personal level *right now*. To have Him and all He can give takes a deep desire for more than what this earthly material life has to offer, and eventually we have to know that Baba can help us acquire everything worth having.

# Chapter 6

## Testing Time - First Visit to Baba

*"No one can come to Puttaparthi unless I call him. I call those who are ready to see Me. Of course, there are different levels of readiness."*
- Sathya Sai Baba

I suppose most of us have made poor decisions in our past that still make us cringe. What I'm about to share is one of those situations. I've kept it buried for almost thirty years. The sole purpose in bringing it up now is to give you one more instance of how much Baba is willing to help on a personal basis, yet without interfering, as He holds the door wide open to personal growth.

The benefit of self-inquiry (taking a close, unbiased look at my attitudes and behavior) is to see the truth about myself, so I'm aware of what adjustments are necessary to be able to reach my goal. That's where spiritual tests come in. They're not usually easy and sometimes the outcome isn't only surprising, it really does sting. Along the lines of a popular quote, spiritual tests are mandatory, but suffering is optional. To be honest, I don't go *looking* for spiritual growth opportunities but they manage to find me anyway. I vaguely remember an old Hindu story about someone being offered a wish from God for anything he wanted. What did the man ask for? Hardships for the rest of his life so that he would always have God on his mind and in his heart. Me...not so much.

Whether His attitude is humorous or totally serious, Baba often reminds me that He knows all of my spiritual areas that still need work. Although the tests are mine alone to take, He sometimes gives me a 'Heads up!' to buffer the potential (and optional) suffering. Regrettably, these forewarnings don't always make it through my thick skull in time. I tend to notice them most often in hindsight. In a cautionary vein for this test, Baba gave me these two separate dreams well in advance, which provided many clues as to what I was going to be confronted with.

Baba dream, May, 1989 – I was in Saratoga Springs, home (in real life) of my alma mater. Folding chairs were set up under a white tent. I could feel the anticipation and excitement in the air because Baba was coming. After finding a seat I glanced around to see if there was anyone I knew in the audience and was amazed to see my father. I think of him as being very narrow-minded and egotistical and he never saw Baba for who He really is. Baba's arrival was scheduled for 8:00 a.m. and it was already 8:25. My father was also exceptionally impatient, so it was no surprise when I heard him ordering the person sitting next to him to go and get his ticket back because he wasn't waiting any longer. Baba hadn't shown up when He was supposed to so he was leaving.

Then Baba walked in, *so* beautiful and loving and gracious. He looked over the crowd and seated Himself in a folding chair just a few feet away from mine, facing me. Our eyes connected and in that exquisite moment He confirmed without words that He understood everything and that I had His total acceptance and unconditional love. He told me that He'd chosen to sit near me because my aura was the brightest. Stunned to receive such a compliment from Him, my brain seemed to turn to mush. Without thinking I just blurted out that I meditate, as if that was the reason. Even before the sentence was out of my mouth I knew that my response was lacking. If my aura was brighter it was because I'd been working harder (doing sadhana) to exert more self-discipline on many fronts and my love for Him and others had grown in the process. His eyes held mine and we both spontaneously smiled at one another. We were good. No matter what idiocy escapes from my mouth, He knows the truth and what's in my heart.

Other people started interrupting our moment together and I found it irritating, but then Baba turned His attention back to me. Telepathically He commented, "So, *you're* coming to visit *Me...*" referring to my actual upcoming first visit to His ashram in India with a group from our Sai Baba Center. Aloud He said with such innocent concern, "But how will you find Me? You don't have my phone number!" What? Of course I didn't have His phone number, none of us did but I'd be in His ashram! How could I *not* find Him? He chuckled. I didn't get the joke but joined Him in feigned amusement anyway, confidently assuring Him, "Oh, I think I can find You!" I woke up *so* happy that we'd connected and He'd acknowledged that I was coming to visit. Little did I know at the time as to what I was in for.

Baba dream, August, 1988 – This warning dream, also referring to the trip, occurred almost a year before actually seeing Baba in person in India and was also long forgotten when I needed it most. In this scenario I'd gone to see Him in a place that reminded me of the annual Sai retreat camps I've actually been to in the Poconos. I was with two college friends, Diane and Libby, and we were heading back to our cabin together. Suddenly Baba was there and walked right up to us and started a conversation. It was so unexpected and we were thrilled that He'd come directly to us in person.

He told us how happy He was to have us there and wanted us to know that even though He might not be available to us every day in person, He would know everything that was going on at all times. Then he posed a question for each of us to answer. "Will you still love Me and have trust and faith in Me, *no matter what (happens)?*" My first thought was *Uh-oh, there's a test coming.* Still, I answered immediately with complete confidence, "Yes!" My friend, Diane, wavered. "Well..." she whined, "If you disappoint me, how can I still believe that you're God?" That was the dumbest answer ever! The thought in my head was loud and clear: *YOU IDIOT!* Baba then left us and we discussed His question at length as we continued on to our cabin. Actually, I did most of the talking. What does having our desires and expectations met by Baba have to do with *His* divinity? Does the sun not exist anymore because we can't see it on a cloudy day? How can we understand His actions? He has the *whole* picture for all of us and we don't! Granted, He does often fulfill our desires, but in the long run Baba is here for our *benefit,* to help us grow spiritually. If we don't keep uncovering more truths about ourselves, how can we make changes to bring out more of our divine essence? Baba is always the same embodiment of pure love, whether Diane can see it or not! I couldn't believe how short-sighted she was.

As the dream continued, we arrived at our cabin and after organizing things a little around my bunk, I announced that I was going shopping. Libby informed me that if I did, my bed would be moved outside the cabin. I told her that I wouldn't be able to sleep if it was outdoors. I wanted protection from dangerous bugs, poisonous snakes and passing critters. After some hesitation she capitulated and allowed my bed to stay inside but it was positioned right next to the door and I knew I wasn't completely in the clear; I could still be put out if I wasn't careful.

I checked on my money jar and saw that a lot of what I'd brought with me had been used up and knew that what was left wouldn't cover the whole trip. What should I do? A few options came to mind but not the right solution. More important to me at that moment was my mother's upcoming birthday (in real life). I wanted to be able to give her something special since I was near Baba, and she'd recently had a mastectomy (in real life). That ended this dream.

In September of 1989 I was on my way to India to visit Baba in person for the first time, as part of the inaugural group pilgrimage from the Washington, D.C. area. There were twenty-two of us and our leaders were Sheela for the ladies and Subba Rao for the men, both ideal people to be at the helm. We felt fortunate that they were willing to navigate a group of 'first-time-westerners' to India for Baba's darshan. We were all long-time friends and they'd both been to Baba's ashram many times and had been granted numerous private interviews with Him, which is an exceptionally rare experience that everyone hopes for but very few receive.

In my mind I couldn't have been more prepared for this enormous journey half-way around the world to be in the physical presence of Sathya Sai Baba. I loved Him to bits and had all the recommended essential items packed, along with the booklet of ashram rules. What an opportunity! I was so excited; He'd already transformed and improved my world so much from so far away, I couldn't even imagine how much more spectacular His effect would be in person! At that time, in 1989, I'd already had eight years of getting to 'know' Baba, between all the guidance through His dream visits and the miracles He'd given our family, and from hearing about other devotees' experiences. I'd also read dozens of books by Him and about Him and had gained additional clarity on His spiritual discourses through Viswanathan, our center's president, whom I consider to be the epitome of Baba's pure, loving spirit and teachings.

One quick aside here - Years after taking this trip, a friend who's a psychologist shared her personal theory about a seemingly universal ashram experience 'westerners' goes through. When we make the effort (physically and financially) to go half way around the world to be with Baba in His ashram, we're most likely serious about our spiritual growth. To reward us for our efforts, the process of discharging our personal karmic debt gets kicked into high gear. Consequently, our spiritual growth takes less time to complete (possibly several lifetimes less) and our liberation from the cycle of birth and death is sooner rather than later. Great, right? The bad news is that what we're subjected to is akin to being steamed alive in a pressure-cooker. The heat is turned up and we undergo unwanted sustained pressure, forcing our deepest impurities to seep out and bubble up to the surface, to be skimmed off and discarded. Personally, I can totally attest to the fact that ashram life can give an un-freakin'-believable number of opportunities to skim off layers of ego-causing misery. Gotta say, it would've been nice to know this before the trip!

Between the excitement of being en route to Baba and the fact that I'm a very light sleeper, I was awake the whole trip. The last leg of our flight landed in Bangalore more than thirty hours after leaving D.C. and then we had a three-and-a-half hour bus ride to His ashram, Prashanti Nilayam, the Abode of Peace. My mind was fuzzy and I'd lost track of how many hours it had been since I slept.

Better than a triple latte, I perked up at my incredible stroke of good luck when I boarded the bus to the ashram. I got the very first seat behind the bus driver and had a full, unobstructed view of everything. Our bus barreled through Bangalore alongside auto rickshaws, motor scooters, bullock carts, bicyclists and pedestrians, as well as cars, trucks and insanely overcrowded buses. I even saw one boy on a bicycle pass us with about thirty dead, unplucked chickens stacked up! Traffic lights were merely discretionary. As if there wasn't already enough insanity on the road, signs were painted on the back of many vehicles instructing drivers to "Sound Horn". The cacophony accompanying this overwhelming moving mass of humanity was mind-boggling. When we got to the outskirts of the city the paved road disintegrated mostly into rough gravel. That fact didn't slow down our bus driver! He was heavy on the horn and played 'chicken' with on-coming traffic the whole way. (Harrowing taxi rides I'd had in Italy suddenly seemed like a walk in the park!) Normal breathing gave way to panicked gasps, and alternated with holding my breath. My arms flew out in front of my face several times to brace for the impending fatal impact. After the third involuntary scream and near-miss I couldn't take it anymore; I relinquished my seat and retreated to the back of the bus where I welcomed the obstructed view. My nerves were frazzled; we could've all died! This was not the mental state I planned to be in on my way to Baba!

Due to a glitch in the Accommodations Office there weren't enough rooms allotted to our group, so, until more rooms became available, we had to double-up even more than the usual number of people in a room. I had to share the floor of an average sized bedroom with four other women on the top floor of a five-story walk-up round building. We squished in with our luggage right next to us because there were no closets or dressers or shelving for clothes, as well as no beds. Worst of all, it was at least 100 degrees in the room and there was no air conditioning, only a sporadically working ceiling fan.

We'd arrived in time for afternoon darshan and quickly got ready. After the hastiest shower I'd ever had, I changed into my white cotton salwar kameez and was dripping in sweat from head to toe again before even leaving the room. I'd only been in India a few hours and never, *ever* sweat so prolifically. Every pore felt wide open and was expelling as much as it could...yuck! Some people didn't seem fazed by it and even accepted it as a purification process. HA!

For those who haven't been to Baba's darshan, there's a strict protocol. Things are run in a very precise, orderly fashion. Men and women silently and separately line up to sit in an outdoor waiting area. Shortly before Baba comes out, a seva dal (an ashram-appointed volunteer) walks over to the head of each line holding a cloth bag for the first person in line to select a chit, sight unseen, which looks like a Scrabble tile, only with numbers instead of letters. The number on the chit determines the order in which your line files in to sit on the floor in the darshan area. Supposedly, the lower your number, the closer and better your darshan will be. If Baba should tell any member of your group to "Go!" during darshan, the entire group has permission to quickly go sit on the veranda until He finishes walking among the crowd. Then they're escorted into the Interview Room where He gives more personal attention and sometimes answers individual questions.

Our group got a very good number. We were all set! We were going be sitting near the front, hopefully very close to Baba, where He could easily notice us. At this point I think it had been close to forty hours since I'd slept, but the adrenaline rush in anticipation of finally being in Baba's physical presence temporarily obliterated all traces of sleep deprivation.

Even before Baba came into view, His energy could be felt. I've been to many 'sacred places' in the world. They all have a noticeably charged, unique atmosphere that distinguishes them from normal places. In Baba's ashram there's an area that surrounds the mandir, the temple where He occupies a small room from which He emerges for darshan. (In the '90's it was covered and transformed into Sai Kulwant Hall). It's where people sit in silence and wait for Him. This place emanates the deepest, most profound serenity and sense of peace I've ever experienced anywhere. Millions of people come here every year, individually or in groups, from all around the world. I don't think you could find greater diversity of cultures congregated in one place, all sitting silently, each hoping for the same basic thing, to be given the blessings of pure divine love, grace and the guidance of Sathya Sai Baba.

All trivial, flitting thoughts evaporated effortlessly for me here. I could exhale, *really* exhale! For a few precious moments it's as if all the 'hats' I normally wear, (daughter, wife, mother, store owner, etc.) come off and I am simply my Self. Not a body, not a personality bearing a particular relationship with others, but I am the essence beneath all the roles I play. I'm aware of my intrinsic connection to the infinite, supreme consciousness that pervades everything. These moments of bliss and perfect equilibrium are truly heaven on earth to me.

The soft Indian flute music wafting through the air stopped abruptly. Out of nowhere a relatively cool breeze picked up. Then Baba silently walked out and all eyes were riveted on

Him. I watched, mesmerized at how gracefully and gently He moved among the crowd, accepting letters from some outstretched hands, making a comment or smiling at others and materializing vibhuti through His fingertips for a few.

We weren't far from Him but He didn't glance in my direction as He walked toward us. When He passed by without making eye contact or acknowledging me at all, I had an overwhelming urge to jump up with my arms outstretched to Him and shout out, "B-A-B-A! LOOK! I made it; I'm HERE!" He acknowledged others in our group but strode past me, seemingly unaware of my presence and my attention on Him and He continued walking, now with His back to me. Replacing all my excitement from just seconds before, a huge lump in my throat formed and my vision blurred from tears welling up. I sat there motionless, hurt and confused. Baba didn't welcome me to His home after I came *all this way?* We were so close physically I could almost reach out and touch Him, and He didn't even look at me? Why? What's wrong?

If I'd recalled the dream with Him and my *college* friends at that moment, it might have registered that this trip was not likely to be all fun and games. I was in a special place with them for a specific reason, implying an educational setting, a place and time for learning and growth. His question, "Will you still love Me and have trust and faith in Me, *no matter what?*" should have been a big hint. For the first time ever, Baba disappointed me. Was I really okay with that? Something else I should have noted (if I'd remembered the dream) is that I didn't have enough money to cover my expenses for the entire trip. Good karma is often compared to having money in the bank. Smooth sailing, easily obtaining what you want without hardships, can be seen as a result of having accrued good karma and in the dream I saw that I didn't have enough for the entire trip. There had to be a reason for this apparent rejection but I didn't have a clue that it was a test of faith because I didn't remember the dream.

We sat cross-legged on the ground for an interminable number of hours in the heat, between waiting for darshan, having darshan and singing bhajans after darshan. Afterward we rushed to and through dinner because we each still had to purchase a foam mattress to sleep on. Time wasn't on our side; we had to be back in the room for 'Lights Out' at 9:00 p.m. and it was already almost sunset. Probably from my lack of attention due to sleep deprivation, it wasn't until I turned to leave the bedding stall that I noticed that the women I'd come with were gone. Actually everyone was gone. Glancing around I saw that the sun had set, the streets had emptied and sellers from surrounding shopping stalls were closing up for the night. The only sound I heard was the whiny buzz of mosquitos chowing down on my legs. Uh-oh...

Where was my room? We'd been in such a rush to line up for darshan that I hadn't paid attention to the location of my room and I have no sense of direction. The only thing I remembered was that it was at the top of a white round building. The adrenaline rush from the trip itself and anticipation of seeing Baba in person was finally giving way to utter exhaustion. I picked a direction based on nothing, with no confidence that I was heading the right way, and left the bedding stall with my mat rolled up under one arm. I surprised myself when I did eventually come across a white round building, several in fact. Choosing the first one, I climbed wearily to the top, hoping it was the right one. It wasn't. I descended back to ground level and climbed up another one to the top floor. Wrong again. I was losing circulation in the arm holding the foam mattress and the night sky was getting darker by the minute. My lower lip began quivering involuntarily as fatigue crashed down on me. I intended to keep walking but I crumbled. Both knees buckled and I dropped down onto the steps, released my grip of the bedroll and cried and cried like I'd never cried before. Some outdoor lights had come on but the whole place was so unfamiliar and deserted and somehow surreal. After the hurtful reception I felt from Baba in darshan, obviously *He* wasn't available to call on for help. I tried to grasp on to facts in my muddled mind: I was half way around the world in a place I'd never been, lost, exhausted beyond words, Michael wasn't with me (he would have taken care of everything right away, with his incredible sense of direction) and there was *nobody* to help me. I couldn't even make a call because *I had NOBODY'S PHONE NUMBER and there was NO PHONE!* More pitiful sobs gushed out until all my tears were spent.

Although I couldn't recall it when it would have made a difference, a year before taking this trip Baba *knew* that I was going to feel lost and abandoned in His ashram and that I wouldn't reach out to Him for help. If I knew that He knew my plight, it would have spared me tons of tears and trauma. In the dream He'd *specifically* asked me, "But how will you find me? You don't have my phone number!"

The prickly tingling of having lost circulation in my behind from the concrete steps impelled me to hoist myself up to continue searching. Rerolling my mat, I trudged on to the next building. Half way up the stairs – a God-send: "SHEEELAA!" I threw my arms around her, holding on for dear life, as my bedroll got away from me again. Between the desperation in my voice and the intensity of my hug, I might have scared her a little. "What? Karen, what's wrong? What happened? Where have you been?"

I thought I'd emptied my reservoir of tears but no, there were still plenty. Blubbering almost incoherently, "I got lost! And didn't know where my room was or where to go…and I couldn't find anybody to help me!" Sobs overtook my words but if I could have continued I would have added "…and I'm *so* hot and *so* tired and I've got millions of mosquito bites on my legs!" Her soft, soothing voice helped calm me. "It's alright, Karen. You're here! Come, I'll take you right to your room." She retrieved my bedroll and insisted on carrying it the rest of the way up the stairs. Grateful, I followed.

With the unnerving and disappointing reception I felt I'd received from Baba, navigating my environment and lack of comforts became my biggest focus, instead of dealing with the fact that my feelings were crushed and trying to get some insight about it. There was so much to deal with in adjusting to ashram life. With the ten and a half hour time change I was only getting about two hours of sleep at night and not able to stay alert during the day. The overwhelming heat was more than I could handle – I think I only stopped perspiring for about two hours (pre-dawn) in a twenty-four hour period. The food wasn't working out - I stayed with my group but couldn't eat most of the food in the South Indian canteen because it was too spicy (I didn't know there *was* a North Indian canteen) and the bakery, which was good, had very limited hours and very long lines. I was also irritated about having to take my damn sneakers off in so many places. Nobody warned me about that and I wasn't prepared for it. I've never been one to walk outside barefoot so my feet weren't conditioned for it. The only time I walk barefoot is on a clean smooth floor indoors. All these issues and others were significant at the time, but the worst was feeling ignored and rejected by Baba. That cut deep and I couldn't see what I'd done to deserve it. To top it off, Subie and Sheela were arranging for us to do seva in the ashram. Just what I needed...someone volunteering my time to do physical labor when I'm beyond hot, cranky, tired and hungry!

About a week later I'd adjusted somewhat and was sleeping longer at night and feeling more awake during the day. One evening when we were outside after dinner, I noticed a tall Australian girl with long dreadlocks standing in the street talking to a friend while munching on a little bag of popcorn. When she saw how I must have gaped at it, and exclaimed in disbelief, "POPCORN!! Where did you get that?" she immediately insisted I take her bag and also gave me directions to the little popcorn stall which was only opened for a couple of hours at night. I couldn't turn it down, even though she wouldn't let me pay for it. I found the stall and bought ten bags to take back to the room! Next door to that stall turned out to be a place that sold cashews. YESS! I also found out that if you run to the bakery in the morning right after bhajans, for a short period of time you can get a baked potato...a *baked potato!* SAI RAM! This level of excitement over a baked potato should have been a big red flag that my head was not in the right place, but I had no idea at the time. Things were starting to look up physically, but becoming even more complicated and confusing regarding Baba.

My involvement in the unexpected highlight of the trip was also indirectly referred to in the Baba dream. I'd brought the letter to darshan that Mom mailed to me to give to Baba. She wasn't a strong believer, but with all she'd been through with her breast cancer, she was open to 'alternative' healing therapies. She'd had a mastectomy and chemo but had just found out that the cancer had returned. Baba accepted her letter and after returning home from the trip, when I called to tell her about it, I found out that she'd had a Baba dream (the only one ever) on the same day He'd accepted her letter. She told me that this dream was unlike anything she'd ever experienced, waking or sleeping. In a rare moment of confiding in me, she admitted that she was overcome emotionally by Baba and automatically fell to her knees in the dream because she knew she was in the presence of God. He produced a waterfall in the dream which flowed throughout her body, inside and out, and she felt that all the cancer cells were washed away. She'd become completely clean. Weeks later (in real life) after receiving an updated set of test results at her request, the doctor was shocked more than Mom. My mother had become completely cancer-free and she remained that way for more than twenty years. The reference in the dream of wanting to give Mom a special gift because I was near Baba (even though I didn't have much money) was clear. If I hadn't gone to see Baba in person, Mom wouldn't have written to Him. My gift to her was special because I was able to hand-deliver her letter to Him and He responded to her tiny grain of faith by appearing to her and curing her cancer.

One day Baba greeted Subie in afternoon darshan and then said "Go!" Subie motioned to Sheela on the Ladies' side. She nodded to us and we all popped up immediately and hurried to the veranda. YES! This was it! We were all going to the Interview Room with Baba!

Our group was ushered inside along with a Telegu family whose daughter was getting married. As I sat cross-legged on the floor only about two feet from Baba's chair, I watched Him materialize a beautiful long necklace from the palm of His hand for the bride-to-be. In the same way a silver container filled with vibhuti came *through His palm* for an elderly woman with cataracts and He gave her instructions on how to apply it to her eyelids. The materializations were astounding yet Baba made it appear completely effortless.

When His attention turned to us, He held His first two fingertips and thumb together and vibhuti flowed non- stop until He'd finished sprinkling some into everyone's right hand. I put all of mine into my mouth immediately. Then He addressed us from His chair and several of us had the additional gift of taking padnamascar, the blessing of touching His feet. He didn't take many personal questions but Baba looked at each of us individually and made a statement that was relevant to that person. To one He spoke of unity through diversity. Here's part of it: "Stars are many – the sky is one. Ornaments are many – gold is one. Sweets are many – sugar is one... Bodies are many – Atma is one." When He turned His attention to me, he recited my favorite quote of His regarding motives and outcomes:

*"If there is righteousness in the heart*
*There will be beauty in the character.*
*If there is beauty in the character*
*There will be harmony in the home*
*When there is harmony in the home*

*There will be order in the nation.*
*When there is order in the nation*
*There will be peace in the world."*

It all appeared perfect. I was in close proximity to Baba. We'd been given the coveted interview. He materialized vibhuti right in front of me and sprinkled it in my hand. I got to stroke His feet and Baba looked into my eyes and spoke directly to me. Most devotees would have been delighted and very grateful for any one of these gifts. The others in my group were positively elated, but I wasn't. The emotional experience with Baba in person didn't compare to the intense connection and love I'd felt from Him in my meditation room at home and in His dream visits. I felt blindsided; it never occurred to me that my experience with Him could be *less* in person in His ashram than in my house, half a world away from His physical form. How could that be? Shouldn't His physical presence emit the most concentrated powerful energy? This wasn't what I expected. I didn't understand, but it didn't seem right to ask anyone in my group about it; they were all so happy with their experiences and we'd been given so much.

Once again, if I'd only recalled Baba's dream before this trip, I would have known what this was all about. How could I have been so quick to answer His question and so sure of myself when my faith in Him had never been tested? Here I thought I was visiting Him with unshakable, unconditional love. Take away some sleep, some food, air-conditioning and a heart-warming welcome and where was I? My ego-filled expectation that I would be given so much more by being physically close to Him was causing me a ridiculous amount of misery and confusion! To add insult to injury, in the dream I'd arrogantly berated Diane for expressing her doubts about Baba if He were to disappoint her. Baba has addressed this subject and the bottom line is that if you come to Him extending your cup to be filled, but it's already filled with your own desires and expectations, there's no room left for Him to fill it with what He wants to give you. I didn't know that I'd come to Him with my cup already full!

Instead of trying to quell all this turmoil by getting Baba's guidance through meditation, and despite the explicit instruction to stay inside the ashram at all times, I ventured out to check out a few little jewelry shops on the main commercial street of Puttaparthi. I wanted to look for some new inventory for my store, as well as find gifts to bring home. From what I saw when our bus first drove into the ashram, it looked like there were lots of cute little shops out there. I didn't see any harm in it and it could be a nice change of pace.

The jewelry shop owners, mainly Pakistani men somewhat younger than me, were extremely polite and friendly and accommodating. I didn't have to take my sneakers off to go in their shops and their hospitality was wonderful. They even brought me a big *cold* bottle of Bisleri which I rubbed on my face and neck before chugging it down, cherishing the condensation on the water bottle in the blistering heat. We had great rapport. They had a lot of fantastic gemstone jewelry and loose stones at outstanding prices. I not only enjoyed doing business with them, it turned out to be a great breather from the confines of the ashram and a respite from my stress regarding Baba. I returned to two of the shops several times and bought a lot more than I expected to.

On the third day before we were scheduled to leave the ashram for Bangalore to catch our flight home, one of the shop owners invited me to join him and his friend who were going into Bangalore later that day for some R&R. I'd confided what a rough time I'd been having in the ashram. I jumped at the chance for a real bed instead of the thin foam mat on the floor and having air conditioning and not having to wait in long lines for food...and not feeling so far away from Baba. I was *so* done with the ashram and still had no insights about my disappointing experience with Baba. I wanted out! I got the name of a good hotel in Bangalore and invited an American acquaintance who wasn't in our group to come, too. I informed Sheela and Subie that I'd meet them at the airport. Although they were clearly concerned about my decision, I didn't let that stop me.

We stayed in a fantastic (air conditioned!) suite for two nights and three days at the West End. Wonderfully elegant and spacious, extra amenities included a gorgeous vase of fresh flowers in the living room and a bountiful bowl of fresh fruit on the dining table, completing the welcoming ambiance. We were happy campers. The temperature was much cooler in Bangalore, too. We savored the extravagant outdoor lunch buffet at the hotel, admired huge brilliantly colored Hibiscus and other tropical flowers on the lush grounds and sipped on cool, freshly squeezed watermelon juice by the pool. We even accepted an invitation from the jewelers to join them for dinner at a rooftop nightclub. My last two days of this trip were indulgently luxurious and relaxing and I hardly had any guilt for having abandoned my group and forfeiting the chance to stay in Baba's ashram as long as possible. After all, He didn't seem to care if I was there or not, and I didn't see a shred of justification for His behavior towards me. It was unfair, it hurt and I didn't want to even think about it anymore.

A couple of other correlations to Baba's warning dreams can be made. First, my father's shortsightedness in making the decision not to wait any longer because Baba hadn't shown up on time. In reality *I* didn't stay in the ashram because Baba didn't 'show up' emotionally for me when I expected Him to and He didn't overwhelm me with love through His physical presence at any point, which I thought was a given (another expectation). I was just as impatient and unwilling as my father to wait for what I wanted. The truth is I couldn't see beyond my bruised ego to love Baba unconditionally, the way He loves me. It completely eluded me that His focus is to give me the opportunity to grow, so my divine nature can flourish and supplant the petty, egotistical 'weeds'.

One final correlation here is the decision to leave the protection of Baba's ashram to go 'outside' to shop. Because of my actual 'outside' shopping in the village, which led to the invitation to go to Bangalore, I left the ashram early, pretty much on my own. In retrospect, there was more than one way I could have been in a vulnerable, unprotected and potentially dangerous situation. In the dream I knew it was a bad idea to sleep 'outside' on my own, but in real life I went anyway. More than once I've wondered just how big a blessing Baba actually gave me when He looked into my eyes, knowingly, and sprinkled His vibhuti in my hand.

At home after the trip I shared many of our group's experiences with family and friends and told them all about being in the Interview Room and the materializations I'd witnessed. As for the overall disturbing experience of disappointment, I kept that to myself. Unexpectedly, it weighed on me more and more every day. Why had Baba done this to me? I couldn't let it go. I had to get this mystery unravelled. It was the only time in eight years, since He came into my life, that I was questioning our relationship.

I found myself mentally reliving the interaction we'd had (or didn't have) in the ashram. It went on for months, with increasing exasperation and sadness as I dug for clues to understand why it all happened. What had I done? Feeling separated from Him was miserable. Finally, as I awoke one morning, the answer clicked into place and I finally deciphered what the whole thing had been about. How could I have *not* seen it? It was so simple: I'd totally failed in my test of faith and love for Baba.

In re-reading past Baba dream journals I'd written down, I finally found both dreams that were meant to help me through it all. So much drama I didn't have to go through...but now I am much more aware of how powerful and blinding the ego is, and how crucial its destruction is. It takes no effort to live with egotistical perspectives of our own making, but in a way, they're like a monstrous octopus whose tentacles will pluck us away from where we want to be and perhaps devour us altogether. They've got to be acknowledged, fought and destroyed. Although I couldn't see that my ego had distorted my perception for quite a while, Baba's test ultimately created a stronger and closer bond with Him than I've ever had. So, as much as I would have preferred to avoid all the pain, frustration and confusion of this test, it was worth it, even if I didn't take advantage of His 'Heads up!' dreams of warning. I can take comfort in that He offered me the opportunity *not to suffer*.

This following dream was very quick and to-the-point, exemplifying Baba's patience while giving me much needed insight.

July, 1998 – Preface: For many years I've subscribed to Baba's monthly spiritual journal, Sanatana Sarathi (The Eternal Charioteer). Up until recently I was anxious to receive them and would delve right in to all the articles. In the last few months, though, I've noticed I haven't been reading them. I look at Baba's full-page picture inside the front cover and read His quotation on the back cover, but the journals have been piling up on the coffee table unread. I'm avoiding them and I don't know why. I meditated on it to find out what was going on. Brutally honest insight came right through. There's a great deal of wisdom contained in those pages but actually absorbing it and incorporating it into my life can be *so* hard to do, sometimes *too* hard to do, and then I feel like a failure. Consciously following a spiritual path can be the most difficult challenge there is in life. So, if I don't feel I'm strong enough to defeat this overbearing ego of mine, if I stop trying to, I can't fail, right? I'm still a good person. Why should I be indirectly reminded every month of my spiritual shortcomings?

In this dream Baba and I were casually sitting together and He was telling me about a new, special grocery store. It was a really impressive one, like a Wegmans. He was quite animated as He talked about it and was using hand gestures, too, like I do when I'm talking excitedly about something. He suggested that we go check it out together right away. Delighted, I immediately agreed. The scene ended and just a second later the whole thing was repeated by Baba, exactly like the first time. The second time I was both a participant and an observer of it all and the conversation seemed rather plastic and had less impact. It wasn't actually worth the level of interest or excitement I'd given it the first time and definitely not a subject worthy of Baba's time. He had many more important things to talk about than this! Baba's message was embarrassingly clear. "If *you* won't come to *Me*, (with an interest in what I've come to teach), then *I'll* come to *you* (at your level of interest)!" *Ouch!*

This brings to mind a section in the Bhagavad Gita (chapter twelve, starting at verse nine) where different ways to reach God are offered to the spiritual aspirant, to make him "very dear to the Lord." Several options are suggested, but after each one there's a back-up plan in case you just can't do it. For instance, "If you are unable to completely establish the mind steadfastly in me" then... and "If in the practice of remembering me you are also unfit" then... and "If also this you are unable to perform" then... I appreciate this attitude! It's quite considerate to have our human frailties taken into consideration. My take-away from this is that there is no requirement or expectation to take on all my spiritual challenges at once. It's overwhelming and will likely lead to a sense of failure. However, it's not okay to give up trying altogether, either. It makes a big difference in the long run to keep on going!

# Chapter 7

## 'Sweet' Leelas

*"Watch – your Words, Actions, Thoughts, Character and Heart. The mind is like a mad monkey. You should not surrender to it...Watch it carefully...and have control over it."*
- Sathya Sai Baba

In a way, it's like a bug that hits out of the blue, but unlike a simple flu, which is uncomfortable and can take you out of commission for a while, this 'ailment' doesn't pass in time with bed rest, antibiotics or extra fluids. It's different. Diagnosing it can be tricky but ignoring it is a mistake. I don't think the people around me are a factor in the timing of it. Michael and I love each other and get along better than any couple I know, but it doesn't make a difference. Being a Mom is fulfilling for me, with all of its joys and most of its challenges, but I don't think that enters into it either. My store, Sunburst Treasures, can be an emotional rollercoaster ride, between very profitable good years and the recession, however the interaction with my customers has been consistently rewarding.

Michael understood and, although he never suffered from it, he could recognize my symptoms. He knew when I needed to withdraw from regular life completely and take off *all* the 'hats' I wear, to not play any role to anyone, but just simply be. It's not a matter of running away from anything, just once in a while the outer personality needs to recede in order to truly recharge internally. I know this might sound indulgent, but for me it's as essential for survival as clean water to drink and fresh air to breathe. Being in a space conducive to merging with divinity, to absorb the bliss and sublime peace of perfect equilibrium... it's crucial to me. Decades before realizing that this renewal can be accomplished anywhere at any time, I thought it was necessary to be in a sacred place (and it does help but isn't required).

It was September of 1993 and things were back to normal in the house. Rebecca, ten at the time, had recovered from her ninth major surgery at Georgetown University Hospital and we'd both made it through the rigors of Pediatric Intensive Care. Michael knew what the trip to Baba meant to me and offered to not only pay for it but take care of our three children and the house while I was in the ashram for almost three weeks. Having his office in the house helped give him the flexibility to accommodate the kids' schedules and he made it all work, from grocery shopping and cooking to chauffeuring them to extra-curricular activities. Even though he had a lot more to shoulder in a day, he took it on with gusto. I knew he could handle it but from everything I was told when I got back home, he really enjoyed it, too. I'm pretty sure that it was only when I was away that Michael felt he had free rein in my kitchen; don't ask me why. He created fresh baked breads from scratch and concocted several (apparently tasty) new casseroles for the kids. Sarah was twelve and a budding chef since the age of six (who, after college graduation actually did go on to culinary school). She gave me a full run-down of the new meals her Dad came up with while I was away.

Michael's parting words and only instruction when he dropped me off at the airport, after one of his wonderful big bear hugs and a memorable good-bye kiss, was "Get what you need and bring it back with you!"

It was my third visit to Baba's main ashram, Prashanti Nilayam. As you're aware, the first trip was very difficult and a huge test of my faith in Him. On the second visit I found that, despite unbearably hot temperatures and sparse accommodations, being with Baba in darshan can be the most inviting place I've ever been in my life. If you pay attention there's a noticeable purity of energy inside the ashram. When my taxi passes through the main gate I get the feeling that I just crossed home base and I'm safe!

In addition to volumes of lengthy spiritual discourses, Baba has given great little aphorisms, too. If you've ever been in a Hard Rock café, which was originally owned by a long-time Baba devotee, you've probably seen one of them in print near Baba's picture: "Love All, Serve All". Another is "Help Ever, Hurt Never". They make sense and they're good little reminders. One of them, though, that was on my mind just before this trip has always bothered me. It's "Love My Uncertainty." Maybe because I've been a control-freak for as long as I can remember, but this one seems rather foreboding to me. My knee-jerk reaction is to back away with caution. *Uh-oh...what's gonna happen and can I make it through?* Until I'm hit with the unexpected, I don't notice how much I love embracing the familiar and how risk averse I actually am. I was not looking for spiritual growth on this trip, just some bliss.

Dealing with logistics in India can be more of a creative challenge than anywhere else I've been in the world, often requiring much more patience than I'd normally exert in a day. No matter how unsettling things can get, though, Baba always manages to 'have my back'.

While pushing my heavily laden luggage cart out of Customs that early September morning, I spotted Ahmed waiting for me. He managed to be in the front row, which was at least fifteen deep, standing with hundreds of others who were also waiting for deplaning passengers. At that time he was simply a taxi driver for Babu's Taxi but driving was only one of his substantial talents. Since we first met in 1989, I'd discovered that he's not only fluent in seven languages, his general street knowledge, resourcefulness and trustworthiness are all outstanding. This, along with his quietly optimistic, friendly disposition has led us to several productive excursions outside the ashram that I wouldn't have undertaken otherwise.

One time, lugging my biggest old green American Tourister (before the wheels), full of clothes and toys that my children had outgrown, Ahmed brought me so I could deliver the gifts personally and meet my sponsored child through the Christian Children's Fund. I had the name of the village they lived in but didn't realize it was so tiny and remote. It wasn't even on a local map. As it turned out, the drive was many hours away from the ashram but Ahmed managed to not only find it but also be a great interpreter from Telegu to English. When I was interested in buying high quality star rubies for my store at really good wholesale prices, Ahmed found me a ruby stone cutter located in another miniscule, rural village hours away in the middle of nowhere. Sitting in a tiny hut, shoeless, cross-legged on the floor, again with him as my interpreter and assistant, I shopped, big-time! When I wanted to visit the Shiva temple in Chidambaram and my bus in Bangalore was cancelled due to a late monsoon downpour, Ahmed rebooked my ticket at the bus station during that torrentially rainy night, rerouting me through Pondicherry and then connected me by taxi through a hotel there to reach my destination. The list is lengthy but the bottom line is that Ahmed is my 'person' in India when I do anything outside the ashram and he's become a great friend since we first met in 1989.

We greeted each other among the throngs of people pouring out of the airport and he nodded at me in recognition with a warm yet reserved smile. "Hello, Ma'am. Very good to see you again." I responded with a spontaneous motherly hug. "Ahmed! Hi, Honey! How've you been?" He informed me, proudly yet bashful, that he'd been married for almost two years and had a six-week old daughter since I'd been there last and they were all doing well.

I watched him arrange all my luggage into and on top of his compact, rather flimsy-looking little Tata, with the precision of putting together a jigsaw puzzle. He brought me up-to-date on Baba's whereabouts and I came to find out that Baba was *not* in Prashanti Nilayam. What? He's *always* in His ashram when I visit! Even though in my heart I know Baba is divinity in human form, sometimes the maya lulls me into thinking that when I go visit Him in person, I'm just visiting my very best friend at His house. How can He not be home? It never even occurred to me that He might not be there when I arrived, but He'd gone to Whitefield to the campus of the undergraduate boys' college, about an hour's drive from Bangalore.

*Oh, no...one of those "Love My Uncertainty" moments.* I cringed. In our family Michael has always been the 'go with the flow' person. I'd planned on being in Prashanti Nilayam, the Abode of Peace! I'd never been to Whitefield but it was widely known that they had very few rooms to accommodate visitors. Ahmed had checked on it just before picking me up and confirmed that there were no rooms available there. Hotels near the boys' college didn't exist yet and I didn't know anybody there I could stay with. If I was staying in Prashanti Nilayam the cost would have been about $1.00/day for a room. Now it was necessary to find a decent, reasonably priced 'western' hotel (meaning an American bathroom; I can't deal with the 'eastern' porcelain hole in the floor). Who knew how long Baba would stay at the college? I might need a hotel for the duration of the whole trip. The expense of a hotel room for two-and-a-half weeks was not in my budget. As it turned out, Ahmed knew of a place and I was unpacked and settled in an acceptable, very reasonably priced 'western' hotel in Bangalore before lunchtime. We'd have an hour commute each way from Bangalore every morning and afternoon for darshan but it was do-able. Relieved, I felt I'd dodged a bullet with "Love My Uncertainty."

The area where Baba gives darshan at the college is significantly smaller in size than Prashanti Nilayam. Even though ashram protocol is still strictly adhered to with the separation of men and women for darshan and meals, as well as modest dress and total silence during darshan, the atmosphere somehow feels more casual and relaxed here. I also noticed that Baba seems more playful. For the first time, I witnessed a few devotees in the crowd hold up a tray of individually wrapped candy for Baba to bless as He walked by. Much to the surprise and delight of the audience, Baba would stop in front of the tray extended to Him and sweep up an overflowing handful of wrapped hard candies and toss them into the crowd. It was fun to watch. He hardly moved His arm, yet the candies seemed to explode out of His hand and were propelled dozens of yards into the crowd, fanning out in all directions. When the women reached out and caught one, sometimes you could hear a little squeal of delight escape amid the silence.

The next day was going to be Ganapati Chaturthi, Ganesha's birthday, a special festive day when negative traits and problems are surrendered to Ganesha, the aspect of God that removes obstacles. After darshan everyone's individual clay Ganeshas, mentally filled with the stuff they wanted to get rid of, would be ceremoniously carted off and released into the river, to be forever dissolved. It's a surprisingly cleansing and uplifting experience. I'd had one previous experience of it in Baba's ashram and the memory from two years before in Prashanti Nilayam returned.

At that time, the day before the big festival, I'd suffered a touch of heat sickness, with diarrhea and no appetite. On the morning of the festival I was determined to go to darshan but still felt a little weak and hadn't eaten in more than twenty-four hours. There wasn't anything I could do about it. The canteens didn't open for breakfast until after darshan.

Thousands were in attendance and yet it was incredibly quiet. A soft pinky-peach glow in the sky from the sunrise gave the mandir a pastel, fairytale quality. The children from Baba's elementary and high schools were also permitted to come for darshan on this holiday and were all dressed in fresh white cotton uniforms. You could see their excitement and sheer joy in their faces.

Near the end of darshan Baba gave a signal to someone and several enormous silver bowls were brought out, each requiring two people to carry, and they were brimming with hundreds of ladhus. They're scrumptious, round sweet treats that are made with chickpea flour and cardamom and they were going to be distributed to the children. Even though it was wonderful to be part of this celebration, I couldn't ignore the waves of nausea from hunger that were increasing and I could tell that my blood sugar level was way too low. Suddenly overwhelming, it became clear that I was only a couple of minutes away from passing out. Urgently, I called out to Baba in my mind, *I don't want to leave, but I'm just so hungry, Baba, I can't stay.*

I looked on both sides of me to see which route would be the quickest for getting out of the darshan area. The line of women I was sitting with cross-legged on the floor was dauntingly long in both directions. I glanced over again at Baba, not knowing what to do, and noticed Him speaking to the teacher who was supervising the ladhu distribution. Instantly ladhus started being given out to *everyone* in the audience. This was highly irregular! Excited murmurs went through the crowd. My friend and roommate, Linda, was sitting a few rows in front of me and just a few rows in front of her was one of the ladies distributing ladhus. For some reason she handed Linda two of them instead of one and without a second's hesitation Linda turned and reached as far as she could towards me and I did the same. Even with thousands of people in the crowd, a ladhu was in my hand *less than one minute* after mentally calling out to Baba in distress, needing food. I devoured it through tears of gratitude and immediately felt the lightheadedness and queasiness subside.

So, here in Whitefield with Ganapati Chaturthi only twenty-four hours away, I loved the idea of preparing a platter of candy for Baba. It was such a rare opportunity to give Him something, even if it was just a little sweet, and certainly a lure almost guaranteed to bring Him close to me in darshan the next day.

I strolled down an outdoor corridor of little shopping stalls and found one selling stainless steel plates and containers. Carefully inspecting all the possibilities, I selected the perfect stainless steel platter. Continuing on, I found and compared the best looking and most beautifully wrapped little hard candies. Back in my room it took me the better part of an hour to arrange them all, meticulously placing each one to form conical, symmetrical layers. I was really pleased with my efforts; the arrangement was perfect.

At 6:00 A.M. on the morning of Ganapati Chaturthi, with both arms protectively wrapped around my large round candy tray, off to darshan I went, feeling a little buzz of excitement at the outstanding prospects I had of Baba coming right over to me. It really was the loveliest tray of candy.

The dais was decorated with an enormous profusion of fresh flowers and garlands and an ornate silver and maroon velvet chair was placed in the center for Baba. Students from the college paraded in, all playing instruments and chanting ancient Sanskrit prayers. Baba looked particularly radiant as He scanned the crowd, just beaming the most joyous, tender loving energy to us all.

I'd been getting fantastic spots for darshan, usually between lines one and four, plenty close enough for Baba to notice me and easily reach the candy. For the first time ever, on that particular morning, the number drawn out of the bag for my line was number twenty three. *Twenty three!* If you've never been to Baba's darshan, being in the twenty-third line to file in to be seated means that probably more than a thousand people will be closer to where Baba is likely to stand than you will be. Truly stunned, I sat there cross-legged on the floor holding my candy platter on my lap, straining to catch a glimpse of Him but it was practically impossible because of the distance. How did this happen? I put serious time and effort into this; I thought He'd like it. *Line twenty three?*

My confusion forced me to mull things over to find a reason, to make sense of why this had happened. I believe there are no 'accidents' so I had to figure it out. Finally the light bulb went on and I recognized my faulty thinking. 'Lure'

Baba into coming over to me? How could I have even thought of trying to manipulate Him? Sathya Sai Baba, the omnipresent, omniscient, omnipotent Cosmic Avatar of the Age! The idiocy of my plotting hit hard. How ridiculous of me, how conniving and embarrassing! A huge wave of remorse washed over me. I felt so stupid, not only for my strategizing, but for having caused myself to lose the opportunity to give Him something. Baba is always giving me so much.

Resigned to the fact that I'd really blown it, I let my head drop, dejected, knowing that I wasn't going to receive His attention during this darshan. Resting my eyes on the candy platter still perfectly arranged sitting in my lap, my hand instantly flew to my mouth to stifle a gasp. *Oh my God!* Sitting on the top layer, with everything still perfectly arranged, one candy wrapper was neatly and totally unwrapped, showing teeth marks where a bite had been taken, leaving the other half in the wrapper. No human hands had touched this candy since I'd arranged it! *Oh my God! OH- MY- GOD! HE TOOK IT! BABA ATE A PIECE OF THE CANDY I BROUGHT FOR HIM!* I wanted to shout out loud at the miracle I was witnessing. Furtively glancing at the women on both sides of me, I wondered if they'd seen anything. Neither of them noticed me or paid any attention to my candy tray.

Baba hadn't physically come anywhere near me or even glanced in my direction, but it didn't matter! He knows my heart! He knows *everybody's* heart! Even though I'd muddied my good intentions with egotistical childish antics, He understood why and did accept what I wanted to give Him, and He did it without allowing my ego to get any more inflated! No one else knew! It's been about twenty five years now since this 'sweet' leela and I still have the other half of His piece of candy. This experience and many more have made His declaration, "Love My Uncertainty" take on a new tone that isn't as intimidating. Now I think of it more as: *"Don't worry or be afraid! Be open to new possibilities!"*

# Chapter 8

## Divine Matter

*"Do not crave from me trivial material objects, but crave for Me... Not that you should not receive whatever objects I give as signs of grace... It is to mark the bond between Me and to those whom they are given... That grace is available to all who call on Me in any name or form, not merely to those who wear these gifts. Love is the bond that wins grace."*
- Sathya Sai Baba

There are likely millions of miraculous gifts that Baba has materialized for people since He was a teenager. Sometimes they manifest through His hand, but as you've read just from my experiences, more often they appear in other ways. No matter how His miracles and presents manifest or what their material value, He emphasizes that their true value is the connection they make between Him and the receiver.

One thing He's materialized often is known as vibhuti (pronounced 'vi', short 'i', booty, accent on 'boo'). It's a light, powdery ash that sprinkles out from the tips of His fingers and on rare occasions it spontaneously appears on His pictures. Here's a quick synopsis of what Baba says about it.

> *"Vibhuti is the most precious object in a truly spiritual sense...It represents the burning of desires that agitate the mind and cause confusion. When there is no desire to warp the mind love will be full and true. What greater offering can you give to God to glorify Him than the ash signifying your triumph over desire?"*

Another materialization connected to Baba is called amrith ('a' pronounced as a short 'o' as in Mom, short 'i', and silent 'h'), translated as divine nectar or immortality gaining nectar. It's a liquid similar in consistency to honey but it has a fragrance that's not entirely identifiable. I can't find the right adjectives to describe it but qualities come to mind – purity, tenderness, unconditional acceptance. When I breathe in its fragrance I burst into tears and I don't know why (and that's never happened with any other scent). A little amrith on my tongue produces indescribable joy in my heart and I can physically feel something happening inside me; I just don't know what. Who knows, maybe it *is* from a higher realm than our physical plane. If I let myself daydream on 'what ifs', I'd like to imagine what the world might be like if everyone could take in a little amrith.

Whether you have an opportunity to visit Baba in person or not, there is a place you can go to witness both of these manifestations. What I'm about to share here are not one-time events produced just for me. They've been happening consistently for dozens of years and I have no idea how many have witnessed them, but that doesn't make them any less astounding or miraculous.

From what I've been able to gather, after losing his parents at an early age, a person by the name of Halagappa basically grew up as an orphan. Over time he found work but it didn't pay enough for him to survive and he became a petty thief. At one point he went to Prashanthi Nilayam, Baba's main ashram, and earned the disreputable label for himself of 'baggage lifter'. After personal interaction with Baba he swore off stealing. With Baba's instruction and help, he founded the Srirangapatna orphanage in 1984.

Halagappa made a shrine room dedicated to Baba which has several large framed pictures of Him in it. I'd heard that some of these pictures are almost completely covered in materialized vibhuti and that it actually 'grows' right on the pictures. Logically this doesn't make sense, but if it were true I wanted to take advantage of the opportunity to see it for myself while I was in

India. The trip was almost a six hour drive away from Baba's ashram on the Mysore-Bangalore Road, just a few miles north of Mysore. Ahmed knew it well and told me that he'd personally brought hundreds of people there over the years.

It was a normal sweltering sunny day when we arrived that afternoon in September of 1993. I asked Ahmed to come in with me. Pleasantly surprised, he immediately consented and thanked me. I was surprised to find out that of all the trips he'd made transporting people to the orphanage, he'd never been invited inside before. I think he was almost as excited as I was that we might be about to witness a miracle. He offered to carry my hefty L.L. Bean canvas tote that I'd brought filled with children's books and small toys to donate.

After being cordially greeted at the door and introducing ourselves, I obliged the housekeeper's request to leave my Nike's outside the door before coming in. We were ushered through a spacious foyer to the shrine room and she went to find Halagappa. The children were at school and there were no other visitors at the time. The energy was calm and welcoming and the whole place was refreshingly cool as we padded quietly across the terrazzo floor in bare feet. Entering the shrine we immediately saw all the framed pictures of Baba covered in vibhuti. It was true! Some were hanging on walls, others propped upright standing on the floor. One of them was completely covered in a thick layer of vibhuti except for Baba's face. What I was looking at was difficult to grasp mentally. The vibhuti was covering the *outside* of the framed glass surface! How is that possible? Vibhuti is a very light, powdery ash. It doesn't stick! How could it cling on top of a smooth surface of glass that's standing vertically? How was it defying gravity? When Halagappa joined us I asked him about it and he had no answer except to say "Swami's grace."

We had a pleasant, comfortable conversation and he was appreciative of all the toys and books for the children. At one point he stood up to get a piece of paper and motioned for me to come over to the most vibhuti-filled photo of Baba. He slid the edge of the paper up the glass several inches, causing about two tablespoons of vibhuti to tumble onto the paper, which he folded into a makeshift envelope and gave to me. I saw the clear glass underneath where the vibhuti had been removed by the paper, showing more of Baba's orange robe in the picture. Incredibly, none of the remaining vibhuti on the picture spilled or moved at all. I was stunned and didn't know what to say except for a heartfelt "Thank you!" He turned his attention deliberately back to the picture and said "Look." I followed his eyes. From the area where he'd taken the vibhuti a light new layer was filling in. I just kept staring at it while the vibhuti continued to coat the clear area and in less than five minutes it was completely filled in again! You couldn't tell that any of it had been removed. The vibhuti *grew* right back and I watched it happen! Is that possible? NO, of course not! Did it happen? YES, it absolutely did!

I'd like to mention here that in my experience with vibhuti, it's actually more than a spiritual symbol. It can be physically and emotionally helpful too, depending on what's needed. Although you wouldn't normally think of ash as having value, many people who use it consider it priceless because of its source and its effects. I've had countless experiences of its healing ability under different circumstances. Here are just a couple of instances of the physical effects it's had upon me.

In the mid 80's I caught strep throat and at the time had no medicine for it. I hadn't been feeling close to Baba in a while and (maybe because I was under the weather) I impulsively called out to Him telepathically to ask if He would let me feel His presence. He's so comforting. I dipped my little finger into a tiny jar of vibhuti and took some on my tongue. In less than ten seconds *all* the pain in my throat completely dissipated and never came back. Although it hadn't occurred to me to ask Him for relief, He showed me that when I call out to Him in need, His response is immediate and full.

After Michael's passing in 2008 there were instances where my grieving was so intense, my emotional distress escalated into severe physical pain in my chest and I had difficulty breathing, as well as excruciating back spasms. The only remedy that calmed it down was Baba's vibhuti and, like in the other instance, it also worked within just a few seconds.

Halagappa was happy to share the grace that Baba had showered on him and it showed through his attitude and generosity. After giving me the vibhuti packet he brought my attention to an average-looking stainless steel pitcher that was about a foot tall. He explained that Baba had given him a small oval ceramic piece with His picture on it, about an inch in length and had told him to place it in the bottom of the pitcher. When he did so, many decades ago, the pitcher filled up with amrith. Thousands of people have come to witness this phenomenon over the years and have tasted it and many have been given some to take with them. This is actually two separate miracles; first, the spontaneous creation of the amrith and then, after all these years, the pitcher has *never run out!* Now why should you or I believe that it's miraculously manifested and that it never runs out?

Halagappa took the ceramic piece out of the pitcher, placed it in my right hand and told me to watch it. While observing intently, it became necessary to cup my hand more and more to keep the flowing amrith from spilling over! He then told me to pour it into my other hand, keeping the ceramic in the same hand. I did. My right hand filled up again, completely! I was speechless. The amount of amrith between both hands was dozens of times the size of the ceramic oval! Ahmed ran out to the car to bring back a container I'd brought along (just in case...) so I was able to take both handfuls with me.

Halagappa seemed pleased and helped get every drop of it into my container with his little spoon. He confided that even though the pitcher never runs out, when the ceramic is placed in a person's hand, it doesn't always keep producing. To him, the fact that the amrith flowed so profusely in my hand was a favorable testament to my character. Even if hundreds of thousands of others have had a similar experience, these gifts from Baba are extraordinary and readily available to those who find their way to them.

Here are three very quick (energetically 'light') dream visits from Him.

March, 1997 – I was strolling down a busy city street on a bright summer day. As I glanced at a big store-front window display I saw a reflection of Baba in the crowd along with others also passing by. He was beaming with joy and gave me a brilliant smile. I turned from His reflection in the window immediately to look for His 'real' form in the crowd but I couldn't see Him anywhere. Then the dream was over. I think this may have simply been a little reminder of His omnipresence. Whether I see Him in a solid physical form or not, He's always with me.

September, 1988 – In this dream I was sitting in the front row of the bhajan room at our Baba center in Bethesda. I was attempting to focus on Baba's picture, which was in the front of the room facing us, but wasn't really connecting to it. It didn't seem alive like it had on other occasions. Suddenly a brilliant intense beam of white light about three inches in diameter shot out of Baba's third eye (in the center of His forehead). It was only for a couple of seconds and then it stopped as abruptly as it started. In its place there was a clear window and I saw exactly what Baba was doing at that moment. When I awoke, the impression was that when I align myself to Him, there is no distance or separation between us.

May, 1992 – Baba was driving a school bus full of children in this dream. I was watching from my vantage point several rows behind Him. He was so animated and clearly delighted. Racing over bumps and around curvy bends in the road, a wild ride yet He had total control and

I knew I was completely safe. He was terrifically pleased with the whole situation. I wondered, *Have I finally given Baba the wheel? Looks like it...at least for this trip...*

Sometimes, when the odds of something happening are so astronomical, even if it's not an outright miracle, I can see Baba's hand in it, His leela (play). Here's a recent example. Just a couple of days before joining my brother and his family and a small group for a tour of Ireland, the thought popped into my head to check out the possibility of connecting with a Baba group while I was there. Since living in Arkansas I've really missed not having people to sing bhajans with. Energetically, it fills me up like no other music can. Finding Irish Baba devotees and singing bhajans with them could be the highlight of my whole trip!

As soon as I had the thought, though, I almost dismissed it, for many reasons. First, I was travelling with a group by bus from city to city and in looking at the itinerary, I knew we had a very tight schedule, for the most part, a new city every day. It didn't show a 'free' day anywhere and the whole tour was only nine days long. Then, what were the chances that I would even be in the same city as a Baba center? And, if I did find them and was within a taxi ride away, what were the chances that I'd be in the *right* city on the *one and only day of the week* that bhajans were held? The probability of this coming together was laughable.

Stubbornly defying logic, I didn't give up on the idea, though. After doing some research, I discovered that there is a Sai Baba center that's located in Dublin, a city I would be in for *two* days. As it turned out, we had exactly one unscheduled free day for the entire trip, and it was in Dublin on a Thursday. Thursdays are when this Baba group congregates for bhajans! I took their address information to the Concierge Desk and was informed that the Unitarian church I was looking for was *less than a ten minute WALK* from my hotel! YES! Despite *overwhelming odds* against it coming together, Baba fulfilled my wish and I sang my heart out doing bhajans with a wonderful, zealous group of devotees in Dublin! They seemed happy with me, too. One of them told me that I should move to Dublin; they wanted me to sing with them every week!

# Chapter 9

## Detachment?

*"How can you get God's grace without undergoing trials? You know what severe processes gold goes through from the crucible onwards before an ornament is made. There can be no happiness without pain...Pleasure and pain go together in this world."*
- Sathya Sai Baba

Just *thinking* about writing this brings back uncontrollable tears. It's been more than eleven years but it's still too soon. Maybe it will always be too soon. I've been wavering about whether to share this throughout all the years it's taken me to get the other chapters down on paper. Sharing this experience with Baba widens the spectrum of circumstances for you to see His concern and love and how much He can give through His involvement. So, I'm holding my breath and jumping in.

It was just a routine teeth-cleaning appointment that day in March of 2007 when a small growth was discovered on Michael's gum. The dentist wasn't overly concerned but told him to have it checked out by a specialist. We did and were assured that it was highly unlikely that it was cancerous but an appointment was made at an outpatient surgery center. It was a quick procedure and we were back home in a few hours. About a week later we were notified about what they found in his mouth - squamous cell carcinoma. Michael was immediately scheduled for another procedure to remove more tissue along the margins. We were informed that 95% of all people with oral cancer are either smokers, chew tobacco, are heavy drinkers or are black men. Michael fell into none of those categories; he was one of the 5%. After the second surgery we thought it was behind us.

It was a busy time. Flowers for the church, reception and bridal party were still being finalized for our younger daughter's wedding, which was only two months away. It was going to be held in my hometown, Auburn, New York, so that many of the older relatives who wouldn't have been able to make the trip to Maryland could attend. Most of them were there when Michael and I took our vows at St. Alphonsus church thirty years earlier and attended our wedding reception in the same ballroom at Springside Inn. Rebecca's wish for her wedding was simple: to have it be beautiful, traditional and to include lots of family. Michael and I were able to fulfill that wish for her.

Two months after the wedding, longtime friend Shivakumar, an oral surgeon himself, was able to secure an appointment for Michael with a top oral cancer specialist, the Director of the Oral & Maxillofacial Surgery Center of the University of Maryland in Baltimore. Michael's next surgery took more than six hours and significant skin grafting was required. Twenty-six radiation sessions followed. It took a while to catch on but we finally 'got' the code for the comment we heard from several doctors, "Blood supply to the mouth is abundant."

Several months later, almost a year since the cancer was first discovered, his seventh and last surgery took eleven hours and was horribly disfiguring to his face. He was brought home in a wheelchair with a temporary feeding tube still down his throat. The dosage of pain meds he needed made him dizzy and he couldn't walk because they threw him off-balance. A hospital bed with side guard rails replaced ours. A Hospice nurse came to the house daily to check on him, to take his vitals and change the sizeable dressing on his forearm from the skin graft. My first instinct was to run the other way and hide when I heard the doorbell ring. I know, it's crazy, but maybe if I didn't let them in the door, hospice couldn't be in our home or lives...

Sarah was a God-send. She came home from San Francisco to help. Her upbeat, confident attitude made almost everything seem more do-able. Like me, she's also a take-charge kind of person. Whenever she saw me working on household chores she'd stop me. "Mom! I've got this. You go keep Dad company."

As much as I wanted to I didn't know how to be 'good' company. Over the span of months everything had changed. He was still my Michael deep down... but on the surface he wasn't. Between the drowsiness from the drugs and his difficulty speaking from the tracheostomy and feeding tube still down his throat, we had almost no verbal communication. A pen and pad was kept on top of the covers on his bed but he was usually too weak to use them.

I helped peripherally but Sarah took over for the most part with what had to be done regarding his daily care. The stabbing pain in my chest from seeing him suffer and how much his face had been disfigured made it next to impossible not to break down when we were in the same room together. Sitting next to him in a chair pulled up to his bed, I remember him taking my hand through the guard rail and gently patting it, trying to comfort me and show that he knew what I was going through emotionally. Unsuccessfully fighting back tears, I burst out in angry frustration, "Honey! This is *not* in our plan!" He slowly turned his head toward me, apologetically and whispered in a voice barely audible, "I screwed up."

He'd been torn for more than a year between staying in a job that wasn't fulfilling, which paid very well and offered great healthcare, and giving it all up to retire so he'd have time for everything else he wanted to do. I was okay with either choice as long as he was happy with his decision. We'd taken financial risks before and always landed on our feet. He kept weighing the pros and cons but couldn't seem to reconcile himself emotionally to either choice and the stress ate him up, literally.

I don't think Sarah will ever know how much she did to keep us both alive during that time. I went through the motions to keep up some appearance of normalcy but couldn't shake the mind-numbing fog that seemed to envelop me. *This could NOT be happening – really, it couldn't! We were going to be old when we died and I was going first. We'd talked about it; we'd already made plans. We were on the verge of being financially and mentally carefree again! All three children had completed college without a dime of debt. Two out of three were married and had a child of their own. We were very close to paying off the mortgage! Our lives were good; we were set and about to start our next new chapter together, our 'Golden' years!*

Although Michael and I had distinct, separate personalities, somehow, without noticing, we seemed to have intertwined and melded into one in many ways over our thirty years of marriage. We each had strengths that were weaknesses in the other and without thinking about it we automatically adjusted to support each other. It's fairly common among couples with really good, long marriages. The only problem is that once it happens it's almost impossible to separate again and still be left whole without that partner. I could cite hundreds of examples but it's not necessary.

Except for Baba, I don't think anyone on the planet knew me better or loved me more and it showed. Although Michael had an impressive, gallant romantic side, it only took one knowing look from those penetrating eyes of his for me to feel *so* cherished and loved that it took my breath away. Not being allowed to go through this next chapter of life together was not something I could wrap my mind around.

Even with the drugs and liquid nutrition Sarah and I forced through the syringe into the feeding tube that was closing up, we couldn't do much to help him besides give temporary comfort. My son and his wife came home with our year old first grandson, as well as Rebecca and Peter with our six week old grandbaby. We relocated a picture of Baba and our family Ganesha statue from the altar of the meditation room to a narrow table opposite Michael's bed so he could see them anytime. When it was set up I looked over to see if he was okay with it and he nodded almost imperceptibly in approval, grateful to have their images close to him.

In Michael's last couple of days he developed a deep, painful cough. The drugs did next to nothing to help. The feeding tube down his throat made it even worse and affected his breathing when he had a coughing fit. I found myself gasping, too, trying to breathe for him as I stood by helpless to make it better. Laying in my bed across the hall that night (on May 11th of 2008) listening to him struggle, I couldn't stem the unending flow of hot tears. In desperation, I mentally begged Baba to do something. *P-l-e-a-s-e! You know what a good man he is. Don't let him suffer! If he can't get better, take him...just take him, Baba! Please!!!*

A few hours later, almost dawn, I suddenly woke up. It was too quiet, absolutely silent and I knew. Immediately throwing off the covers, I rushed across the hall to his bedroom to check on him. Michael's body was lying in the bed but he had left me. For the first fraction of a second my only reaction was enormous relief that his suffering was done. Baba had mercifully answered my prayer and I was grateful beyond words. In the next instant, though, I envisioned my life as a huge cathedral-style picture in stained glass and I simultaneously watched it and experienced myself shatter explosively into millions of slivers and shards.

Uncontrollable crying and jagged breathing from stabbing chest pains, along with swollen, cracked and bleeding eyelids (wiping away too many salty tears) were just some of the reminders that I'd survived Michael. Months later when I went to a doctor to get a pain-relieving salve for my eyelids, I refused the offer of an antidepressant. Drugs weren't going to make me miss Michael any less. For more than four years tsunami-like waves of grief washed over me almost every day. I never knew what would trigger them or when it would happen. It could be anything, a random thought in my mind or a song on the radio or just noticing a box of his favorite cookies on a grocery shelf. It didn't make any difference, day or night, or whether I was at home or out. I couldn't stand up to any of them. There were times where for many days in a row I didn't leave the house or even get dressed for the day. It was too demanding and overwhelming to pretend to move through the day normally.

I became more and more detached from almost everyone in my life. Years before Michael became ill I came across the idea of the spiritual necessity for detachment from the world. I also found that Buddhism is based on the belief that pain and suffering on earth is a given and that the only way to escape it is to 'detach' from our desires and aversions. Seriously? So should I have loved Michael *less* so I wouldn't hurt so much now? Baloney! None of it made sense and I decided to side-step this aspect of spiritual growth all together. I had enough to work on spiritually and detachment wasn't something I could wrap my mind around. Besides, is 'liberation' *really* all it's cracked up to be?

Baba seemed far away from me since Michael passed. I knew He wasn't 'away' but I couldn't seem to connect with Him. I needed His comfort and strength more than ever but most of the time I couldn't hear Him or feel His presence through all my sobbing.

Both my son and younger daughter kept in touch, but I knew how difficult and awkward it was for them because they didn't know what to say to comfort me and didn't want to accidentally make me cry more. They were hurting, too. Roger, my brother, was so helpful in lots of practical ways but Sarah, my older daughter, was my lifeline. She called me from California at least twice a day. Sometimes we talked about Michael the whole time and sometimes just cried together on the phone without conversation. Sharing our grief wordlessly was an unexpected comfort.

One significant factor that prevented me from joining Michael on the other side was Michael himself. Since I'd developed the ability to connect with those who have passed on, it turned out to be a valuable gift to myself. The first few times we spoke he was gentle and apologetic that he'd caused me so much pain by leaving me. Later on he tried to reason with me to cheer me up. I remember him saying once, "If you check out early you'll miss out on more grandbabies!" He was right; I now have five grandchildren. After several years of grieving, though, I still wasn't improving significantly and after a particularly bad crying jag, again with severe chest pains, Michael's attitude shifted. He became exasperated, I suppose, and he came to me with a firm voice. "Karen! Cut it out! Nobody ever promised you that we'd have til the end of *your* life! Thirty years was *it* for this time! We had a great life together. Remember *that*! I don't want you crying every time you think of me! There are people there who need you and you're *there*, so live!" The problem is he didn't tell me how to *want* to keep living.

I can't emphasize enough how important it is to immediately write down any Baba dream you're given as soon as you receive it because it can sometimes take years before fully gleaning its meaning. This was the case with the first of the three dreams here.

October, 2004 – (almost three and a half years before Michael passed) I was in a place I'd never been before. It looked like a game parlor in the old 'Wild West'. Baba was standing at a round dinner table, holding silverware and arranging place settings. He intentionally looked up directly at me and I could tell He had something serious on His mind. He appeared to be mentally analyzing something. Aloud He said to me, "We'll see..." implying that we'd see whether or not I would be given a seat at the table. "You've got to switch places on Christmas Eve." I knew that I would have to inhabit and then conquer some horrible energy or entity that was terrifying and evil. It was a test of my strength and willingness to take on the fight of my life in order to connect with my Self. Instinctively, I also knew there was only a 50/50 chance of not being devoured and destroyed by this evil force. Realizing the degree of danger I'd be in, I began trembling in fear from head to toe. "Oh, NO-O-O-O-O, Baba!" Between my overwrought emotional state and the tears actually streaming down my face, I abruptly woke up.

Afterthought: It didn't dawn on me until long after Michael passed that my grief and depression and lack of regard for my health had put me on a fast-track of literally dying of a broken heart. This degree of grief could be considered evil because it was destroying my will to live. I was in totally new, uncharted territory, a place which could be extremely dangerous, even fatal (the Old Wild West). Of all the special times of year we celebrated, Christmas Eve was by far the worst in coping with Michael's absence. I couldn't bear it. I was more than willing to die if it meant that he and I would be together again. In this dream Baba wanted me to realize that my debilitating grief was the evil force residing in my body that needed to be overcome so I could 'switch' to my higher Self and allow Christmas Eve to be a loving, cherished and happy time again.

February, 2012 – There was a great deal of symbolism in this dream, which came through loud and clear. It looked like summer and I was standing outdoors alone on fresh new grass. I knew that it was around 4:00 in the afternoon. Normally I wouldn't want to be out at that time of day because it's too hot but I noticed that the temperature was quite comfortable. Behind me, not more than about twenty feet away on a downward slope was a fairly large, unimpressive two story building with tannish/gray drab siding. My vantage point was from the back of the building and I could see the fire exit door. Suddenly the door swung opened and Baba came rushing through, smiling and looking delighted to see me! He'd come down a very long flight of stairs. The main entrance, which I couldn't see, was around the corner on the topside of the building and it was also the front door to a theatre. My initial surprise at seeing Him gave way to child-like exuberance and when I ran to Him His expression became so tender and loving, like I was the most precious person in the whole world to Him! We both spontaneously flung our arms out wide and wrapped each other in a heartfelt hug. Feeling His cheek pressed to mine, I absorbed His love and joy...pure heaven! I woke up from this dream with a big smile on my face.

Afterthought: Several elements seem symbolic so I'll point them out to help pull this message together. Standing on fresh, new grass by myself implies new energy and beginnings, in a new place, alone (without Michael by my side). The time, 4:00 p.m. begins the last third of the day, which could correlate to the last third of my life (if I pass on in my eighties). It was summer and I was outside at the worst (most uncomfortable) time of day – a time and place I would never choose to put myself in, but surprisingly, I was fine. I think the large drab building was me, large and not attractive or a place I would want to be, yet Baba still came out of it in full force (out of me, having resumed my writing of His book). The theatre wasn't in my sight (ready to publicly present to an audience) but I knew it was there for whenever I was ready. Best of all, Baba let me feel how happy He was that I'd come out of it and was in a better place (condition).

September, 2017 – Preface: It's been almost ten years since Michael's passing and I think I've pretty much adapted to my 'new normal'. Recently, though, I haven't been feeling Baba's presence as much, which probably has something to do with the fact that I've drifted again from my commitment to work on His book on a regular basis. Sometimes it feels like it's just too big a project for me. There's so much to rein in...How do I know which incidents are the best to include and if I'm relaying them effectively? I know, it's an excuse, not a justification, but the fact remains that I haven't been as diligent as I could be to finish up the book and that's further reduced the momentum. Last night I decided to sleep with Baba's robe next to me in bed. It was neatly folded in its zip-lock baggie.

In this dream I was walking along in a crowd of others who, like me, had just disembarked from a flight at an international airport. The whole scene was in shades of gray, like the colors of a black and white photo. Suddenly I noticed Baba walking just a few feet in front of me in the crowd. He was in 'real' living color and was wearing His bright orange robe. I realized that even though I hadn't seen Him on the flight, we were on the same plane together! I was shocked and thrilled. "BABA!" I yelled out excitedly. He stopped walking and turned around to face me. He didn't have an entourage with Him and no one else in the crowd knew who He was, so they all kept walking, passing right by Him without a glance. I wanted to give Him a big hug but wasn't sure if it was okay because even in the dream I remembered that I hadn't been working on the book and was feeling guilty about it. What was I doing? Baba has given me the task of sharing His divine light through our experiences together, to help others see that He's here for us *now* to give us love, wisdom and support, so life can be more magnificent than we can imagine. This is big news and I need to get the job done! The scene shifted and there was a gathering of many old long-time friends who are Baba devotees. Baba Himself was there and I noticed that He was holding a toddler in His arms. I knew that the child needed to be fed and offered to take care of it, so Baba entrusted me to do it and He put the child in my arms.

Afterthought: This symbology is obvious. In having been on a big international flight, I'd been on a spiritual or transformational journey and Baba was there, too. Everyone around me in shades of gray indicated that their lives were devoid of the vibrancy and energy that Baba has because they weren't aware of His capacity to infuse their lives with an entire spectrum of light! Setting aside the discomfort of sharing my personal experiences with Him, for the first time, I *want* to let people know about Him, so they can have a more beautiful life 'in living color' too! The baby in Baba's arms is this book. I've always thought of it as my baby. Each completed chapter adds to its size and health. Knowing that the 'child' needed to be fed and that it was handed to me to take care of was a clear message to keep 'feeding' this book with the fortifying nutrition of Baba experiences.

# Chapter 10

## Light at the End of the Tunnel

*"Nothing ever happens without proper reason,
however accidental or mysterious it might
appear."*
- Sathya Sai Baba

This hasn't been brought up before, but it's one of Baba's more dramatic and unorthodox approaches in offering His guidance. Despite the possibility that my sanity could be called into question, I'm sharing this because it reveals one more astounding aspect of Baba's extraordinary nature.

Among the pictures I have of Him in my house, there's a life-size one of Baba's face that I keep on a wall in my bedroom. Starting about a year after Michael's passing, once in a while, Baba *actually occupies the photograph*. His eyes come alive in the picture and He speaks to me telepathically. I understand how incredulous it sounds, but it's absolutely true. If anyone is wondering, no, I don't drink or do recreational drugs. The first few times He appeared, it startled the daylights out of me and my blood pressure skyrocketed, but after the shock settled, I was thrilled that Baba was giving me more personal time with Him. As I said, it doesn't happen often, but the occurrence has become a little more normal over the years and I've come to think of it as a quick 'pop-in' visit for us to touch base when I need His input.

In the spring of 2009 it had been a year since Michael's passing and I wasn't getting a handle on my grief at all. My daughter, Rebecca, suggested that I give myself a complete change of scenery and move to Arkansas to be closer to her. Arkansas! The D.C. area was the furthest south I'd ever lived and sometimes that felt like the Deep South (I never did get accustomed to being addressed as *"Ma'am"*). Me in Arkansas? Not likely, but I decided to ask Baba what He thought of the idea and went over to my special picture to see if He wanted to weigh in on it. He did, but His response baffled me. He looked like He was about to burst into laughter; His eyes positively twinkled with merriment. It was as if He had a fantastic, exciting surprise but He wasn't about to divulge it. Then His expression grew serious and I heard Him say, "Yes! Go!" His attitude was *"Don't you know by now I've got your back?"* It was strange, but between Baba's response and Rebecca's nudges, along with the fact that she and her husband had my new grandbaby, I gave in. With a leap of faith I packed up, sold my home and left Maryland and the D.C area where I'd lived for almost thirty years.

I knew nothing about Arkansas but had heard a couple of stereotypical slurs, which did nothing to make it sound particularly inviting. The reaction from most friends and relatives when I told them where I was going (largely from New York and D.C.) was either "Arkansas? Seriously?" or "You're kidding! Really? You're actually going to go *live* in *Arkansas*?" Rebecca, however, was adamant in her assurance. "Mom, I swear, it's not what you're thinking; it's really nice here! The things you've heard about it aren't in *northwest* Arkansas...and there *are* stores you'd like - even a PF Chang's not far away!" Well, okay. Besides, nothing said I couldn't turn around and leave at any point if I did feel stranded in the middle of nowhere. Arkansas would at least provide a change of scenery so I wouldn't be constantly reminded of Michael by familiar surroundings...and I did have a new grandbaby!

Fayetteville surprised me. Over the past forty years since grad school I've made more than a dozen moves and have lived in many beautiful areas but never any place quite like this. Beyond all its physical attributes as 'the natural state', there's an extraordinary energy here, an undercurrent that's palpable and I think if you're meant to be here, you know it right away. Like me, most of the people I've met

161

here have chosen to come to this area after spending much of their lives in other parts of the country, yet Fayetteville doesn't have that senior retirement community vibe. The energy here is clear and invigorating, creative, vibrant and full of music. It makes me want to take in a deep breath and exhale even bigger. There's a strong sense of community and from what I've seen, the people who live here look happy to be here. Some think it has to do with the energy of the world's highest quality clear quartz crystals that grow in the area but who knows? I have to admit, as I drove through the downtown area, it made me chuckle when I saw the most popular bumper sticker on vehicles all over town: "Keep Fayetteville Funky".

Shortly before moving I called Mary, an old friend and Baba devotee in Baltimore, to let her know my plans. I found out that she'd been to Fayetteville for a dowsing convention... *dowsing!* She gave me the name and phone number of the person in charge of a group that she felt I should check out. Their basic mission is to help humanity and encourage spiritual knowledge, mainly through holistic healing channels. It sounded right up my alley and I knew how badly I needed to be on the receiving end of healing energy. This could be good.

Although personality types and backgrounds are all over the spectrum in this group, collectively they focus their energy and loving intentions on those who ask for help, making a positive impact. Gladys and the group not only welcomed me, they made me feel like part of the family. Spending time with them helped me take the first step in truly adjusting to life as a widow. I found myself in the company of caring people with good energy instead of being alone so much, isolated and cocooned in grief.

Through one long-time member, Pam, an invitation was extended to me to attend a separate weekly meditation circle. It was held in a dedicated room of Passages, a metaphysical bookshop in Fayetteville. The group was started and run by a woman by the name of Itera. All I knew was that she was from Chicago, retired with a PhD in Education and was most recently transplanted with her husband from Orlando, Florida. There were about a dozen of us who attended on a regular basis. Jim, a retired engineer, was also suffering from grief, his from the unexpected death of his son. Although I did more sobbing than meditating for months, I found it a comforting, safe space. There was no pressure to share my feelings and I felt a sense of acceptance. Eventually I became more centered, cried less and became more aware of Baba's comforting presence. Even if I couldn't pick up all the pieces, I did begin to establish a new normal.

One day after meditation we were all having lunch together when Itera started in again. She urged me for the umpteenth time, "Karen, you *really* should go to John." I couldn't help responding with an audible exasperated exhale. My patience was wearing thin. This conversation had been brought up way too often, for almost a year. I knew she wanted to be helpful but she had to stop pestering me; it was irritating. I'd lost count of how many times I'd already told her "No."

"There's no doubt that you think he's the best there is, but I don't *go* to male massage therapists. That's just out of my comfort zone. Nobody but Michael puts his hands on my body."

Like water off a duck, "John is *totally* professional and his touch is incredible. His energy is so centering and healing. I *know* he would be good for you." She'd felt the depth of my grief and her heartfelt concern was very kind but her dogged determination to do something about it was getting on my nerves. She was bugging the hell out of me but still, I didn't want to hurt her feelings. "Thank you. I know how much you care. I'll think about it."

More than a year after that, when Sarah was about to visit from San Francisco, she brought up the subject of massage on the phone. "You know, Mom, I could really use a good massage. I've been spending more time than usual on the computer lately. My neck and shoulders are tight and my lower back is giving me some trouble. Do you know of anybody really good out there I could go to?"

Not from any direct experience, but John came to mind. I dug out his number from Itera and my daughter had an appointment with him. Even though I'd heard nothing but great things about him, with the massages Sarah's had living in the Bay area for years, I was a bit surprised that she was impressed with him.

"Do you know how lucky you are to have John *here,* in *Arkansas*? He got everything I wanted him to and found a whole lot more that needed work too. He really knows what he's doing, Mom. He could be making a lot more money doing this somewhere else. You should go to him."

"I would if I wanted a male massage therapist."

Later that day we were in the produce section of Ozark Natural Foods to pick up a few things for dinner when Sarah nudged me with her elbow. "Mom, there he is! That's John." As I followed her gaze I saw him for the first time. He looked to be in his early forties, was clean-cut with a medium build, quite fit and trim and was wearing a polo shirt and khakis. She headed towards him.

"Come on, let me introduce you." My immediate reaction was a flash of panic and I had no idea why. There didn't seem to be anything about him to warrant it but I wanted to duck out, pronto, in the opposite direction. I couldn't think of an excuse fast enough. *What is my problem?* "O-kaay." I muttered, only because I couldn't think of anything else to say. I followed in her wake with my cart and hoped my voice would sound normal; my vocal chords were constricting.

You know the saying, "The eyes are the window to the soul."? I've found that to be true but in my experience more than 95% of people don't ever actually peer through that window to truly see what's inside another person. Michael did. John does. I can but don't always. Like a deer caught in the headlights, under his calm, penetrating gaze I felt momentarily stunned and frozen and was suddenly hearing my heart pound. A casual observer wouldn't have noticed, but I knew without a doubt that he could 'see' all that was still broken inside me, which was not something I was willing to share. Relying on old acting skills from college, I smiled politely and engaged in small-talk, presenting a calm, pleasant façade, while inside, my mind was frantically yelling out, *Oh my God! Who IS this person, John, and what's he doing here in Arkansas? Am I ready for this?*

At this point it had been four years since Michael's passing and I thought that outwardly I appeared okay. Although my eyelids were no longer cracked and bleeding from constantly wiping tears away, deep down I was nowhere near okay. I believed I was doing a fairly convincing job, though, hiding it for the most part, as long as no one looked too hard. *John does not have the right to see how broken I still am and I know he can!* With a fairly hasty "Good-bye, nice to meet you." I couldn't roll my cart out of the Produce department fast enough. "What d'ya think? Are you going to go to him? You could use a good massage, too." Sarah wanted to know. "He seemed very nice. Maybe I'll think about it." *Geez!*

Itera and I have many noticeable differences, our physiques being just one of them, with her tall, slender, willowy figure and soft airiness in sharp contrast to my almost five-foot-one-and-a-half inch curvy form and passionate, (I wouldn't call it bossy) practical nature. Not exactly two peas in a pod, but we forged a solid friendship and we've had several great adventures together. One day, however, about another year later, when she brought John up in conversation yet again, I hit my wall. Talk about stubborn! Some people just don't know how to take "NO!" for an answer! An idea popped into my head that I thought would finally put this topic to an end for good. If it didn't, worst case scenario, John would know that, although I was better than I used to be, I wasn't actually all that well. So what? I didn't care what he knew anymore. I'd only have a massage with him once, at most, just to get Itera off my back, because apparently nothing else would.

"Alright! The next time you see John ask him if he gives massages with the client fully clothed. If he says yes, I'll go." *There! That should be the end of it!* It wasn't. To be completely honest, I did remove my shoes.

He greeted me cordially in his office and asked me to fill out a standard form before starting our session. A waste of time in my mind, but I accommodated to be polite. On the back side of the sheet was a spot to write in any particular health concerns. I wrote down "grief", with no expectations of him addressing that in any way.

Not that I was overly sociable by any stretch, but real conversation between us was surprisingly easy and comfortable because it turned out that we had a lot in common. He was also born and raised in New York State in a traditional Catholic household with strong Italian influences and, although he looks about twenty years younger than me, there's only about a year's difference in age between us. We both majored in Economics in college, both went on to grad school and both later abandoned careers connected to our degrees (mine in D.C., his on Wall Street). At one point we even both lived in the state of Maryland, less than thirty minutes from one another. The list of our coincidental similarities is very long, some of it surprising, too. For instance, a path of Self-inquiry became important to both of us very early in our lives. He has a connection to Shirdi Sai Baba, I to Sathya Sai Baba, the reincarnation of Shirdi Sai, and we've both spent considerable time in an ashram in India. Both of us love to sing and can lead bhajans, devotional 'call/response' chants, which are most often sung in the Sanskrit language. *What are the odds? ...AND meeting each other in Arkansas!*

Even with remaining fully clothed, John's massages are beyond all others I've experienced, including those from world-class spa resorts. As I'd been told, his touch did melt all my tight, aching muscles and yes, he did go on to dissolve countless other tender spots I didn't know I had. Some top-notch massage therapists are able to attune themselves to their client's body. This ability makes him better than most but not exceptional and John's work is beyond exceptional, truly incomparable.

As I mentioned, when we first met in the grocery store the previous year, I instantly recognized his intuitive ability. So, although it was apparent that I was in dire need of exercise, John also knew that I was *not* open to accepting anybody's two cents about it. I'd lost interest in what my body needed when Michael died. One day, in the middle of working on me, he leaned in close to my ear as if sharing a confidence and whispered, "You know, Karen, your muscles *want* to move." In that unguarded, deeply relaxed, almost mindless state my gut reaction was genuine concern. I thought, *Aawww...and I've been depriving them for so long!* He went on, "You don't have to join anything...just walk, that's all." In that state, at that moment, his advice by-passed my obstinate head and settled straight into my heart. I *could* do this for myself. I didn't know why he would care but he did. Over the years since then I've seen his selfless concern for others in countless practical ways and have realized that it's simply John's nature to be a bright light-worker on this planet.

For the first few weeks I could only manage about fifteen minutes at a stretch but at my best, for a couple of years, I got up to three miles several times a week. I also finally acknowledged that snacking in front of the TV at night was never going to fill the void so I simply stopped. In little over a year I shed sixty pounds, have no more chest pains, have decreased my insulin shots by almost half and have much better control of my blood sugar numbers. As life-altering as this is, it wasn't the greatest aspect of John's influence.

I wasn't familiar with cranial-sacral work and had no clue of what could happen. With John giving it, it's a lot like opening a combination lock to a safe that holds all the most precious treasure you could ever want. His fingers hone in on specific spots on my head and stay there for a few moments with light pressure. Any tenderness I have subsides. He continues on to other points in the same way until finally it's as though an invisible door opens, offering me what I cherish most. John's touch and entire presence seem to disappear, along with my own physical boundaries, and I merge with the most exquisite waves of pure love. It appears in the form of light and this energy flows around me and through me and rejuvenates every cell of me. The absolute peace and bliss and perfect equilibrium it brings dissolves all grief and the illusion of separation from Michael. *THIS* is the love Baba has given me through His dreams and what Michael and I shared together! I never thought I'd feel it again from human hands in this life, so completely cherished and whole and jubilant beyond words. Back to my true center, I'm *HOME* again! It dawned on me that *THIS* was Baba's secret in His picture when we were in Maryland! What a spectacular and unexpected gift!

Absorbing it all through blissful tears and overwhelming gratitude, it literally takes my breath away and that's when I usually become aware of John's gentle but persistent voice, "Breathe, Karen...keep breathing...just breathe." It's not easy. I think I hold my breath

171

automatically because I don't want to let one iota escape!

How does he do it? I've given it a lot of thought and have a theory. With John's level of spiritual purity and selfless desire to help, he can align his divine essence to the essence of me. As tremendous energy pours from his hands into me, it's like a huge lit torch resurging a fire that's waning (from hurricane-force winds). The identical inherent divinity in both of us merges for a moment and mine is amplified without detracting from his light at all. In that moment, in that state, I can absorb the fact that the only thing absolutely real and permanent is divine consciousness. There's nothing to block the acceptance that (the maya) all the delusions and grief, actually the whole play of this physical life, is only relatively real. It *will* eventually dissipate like a dream, leaving only the basis of everything, divine awareness. I'd read about it in spiritual texts but it pretty much went over my head. The search for perfect divine love and bliss is because we *are* perfect divine love and bliss! Baba likens it to a river perpetually moving to try to merge with the ocean. Intellectually I've known it for a long time but absorbing it experientially is something else!

I can finally see that all those unbearably painful years of grief since Michael's passing had nothing to do with how much I love him. Liberation, true freedom through spiritual detachment, *doesn't* mean I should have loved him any less, so I could detach more easily. It's my *attachment to my desires and expectations because* of my love for him that's made me suffer so horribly. My unnoticed selfishness that he continue to stay with me as *my* loving husband and *my* best friend, giving *me* emotional comfort and security and keeping *me* company until I die – these are what caused all the emotional devastation.

I know Michael's well and happy on the other side; we talk often. Because of the depth of our love and the history we've shared over who knows how many lifetimes, though, chances are that if I succumb to the maya, I will suffer from the imaginary gaping wound of our physical separation until we can be together again. However, with the new insights Baba's given me through John's work, Michael's physical absence doesn't incapacitate me like it used to. I am finally in the process of healing.

If there's any silver lining to Michael's death besides my spiritual growth, it would be the people, the many true God-gifts who've enriched my life so much here in Fayetteville. I never would have met them if I hadn't been in desperate need of a change and been given Baba's encouragement to come here, along with Rebecca's recommendation. Michael and I together would never have considered moving to Arkansas.

Itera's undaunted, unrelenting persistence and determination to help me despite my stubborn resistance for years is the pinnacle of all friendships. When it comes to John, I can't verbalize his impact or my gratitude, and now I'm awfully glad that he can 'check-in' to my heart. As a massage therapist he charges fairly for a massage but what he actually gives is priceless.

I'd like to be able to wrap this all up in a bow and say here that, after years of working on it, I have finally mastered spiritual detachment but, no, not yet, actually, not by a long shot. It's still an on-going challenge but I'm better than I was. My reins of attachment to both people and things have loosened some, but the distance between a preference and an attachment can be razor thin. To help achieve it, Baba recommends developing "a ceiling on desires". So many people have gone to Him pleading, "I want peace!" and Baba gives a concise, simple solution. According to Him, when you give up the 'I' (ego) and you give up the 'want' (desires), all that remains *is* peace.

To love without emotional attachment and expectations is new, unfamiliar territory for me and probably for most people in our culture. It doesn't come naturally but in the long run it can make a huge difference. My attachments have given me a comfy sense of security, even if it is false. So, it's not only hard to detach, it can be scary. I've come to think of them collectively as a buoy. I can grab on and hold tight and it might be life-saving for a while if I'm floundering around in deep water alone. It can provide a way to keep my head above water for as long as I can hang on. The only problem is that a 'buoy' can never bring me 'home', no matter how much temporary relief it offers. Baba keeps showing me that the more I let go of my cumbersome attachments (of no permanent value), the easier it is for me to float effortlessly toward shore, encircled by His protective arms, all the way home.

Since regaining an interest in living again, I wondered about returning to the project of writing this book. I'd abandoned it for several years after Michael's death. I'm still not comfortable with opening myself to share these personal experiences with Baba, but I felt I should get His input on the subject, since I've turned a corner emotionally. So I stood in front of His 'alive' picture and asked Him, "If You *really* want me to write this book, to pass on the joy and help You've given me, I need a clear sign that can't be vague or possibly misunderstood." Scrutinizing His face for a sign of life and an answer, it was only a few seconds before my heart leapt as I watched vibhuti materialize in the shape of a heart in the middle of His forehead. Bursting into tears, my decision was made. "Okay, Baba...can't be any clearer than that!"

I'm going to end this chapter with a brief Baba dream. It wasn't the first on this topic but like several others, He gave it to me *years before* Michael died and I wasn't able to figure out its meaning until *years after* he passed. In this one He let me see that He knew all about my upcoming deteriorating health and weight gain that would occur after Michael's death, and that I would have to make a decision about whether I would choose to live or give up and die.

November 25, 2004 - I was part of a small, special entourage who was allowed to travel with Baba. We were in St. Joseph's cemetery, an actual place in Auburn, my hometown. It's where most of my relatives are buried. It rests on a gently sloping hill at the edge of Owasco Lake and has single lane little roads winding among all the well cared for gravesites. In this dream an event had just finished, most likely a burial, but I didn't see an open grave or a coffin. (In real life Michael wanted to be cremated and have his ashes scattered at the Middletown Overlook in Gambrill State Park, so there was no burial site. When his ashes were released, due to a sudden gust of wind out of nowhere, they were taken up into the sky instead of falling to the ground.)

Baba came over to speak to us individually, giving last-minute instructions regarding the next place we needed to go. We each got into our own vehicle but the section of the road my car was parked on couldn't take me to where I was supposed to be. I needed to be up higher on a parallel road in order to follow Baba. It wasn't far from me. I could even see it and it was in much better condition than where I was parked. There was a problem, though - there was no way to drive to that road from where I was. My 'vehicle' (body) was too big and the headstones (death) blocked me from moving forward with Baba. From where I was it would be a very short drive to a 'dead' end. It was obvious that I needed to make a decision about how I wanted to proceed. As reluctant as I was to exert the effort and leave the familiarity of my vehicle, the choice was clear. I got out and *walked* to the road I needed to be on so I could continue to travel with Baba.

Afterthought: Making the decision to follow John's recommendation to start walking was the turning point that helped me lose weight, improve my outlook and restore my health.

# Chapter 11

## More Baba Dream Visits

*"It can never happen as a result of your wish."*
- Sathya Sai Baba

As you've probably noticed, when Baba wants to make a point through a dream visit, it can be quite dramatic. Despite His creative approach, I'm not always a great student; His lessons don't necessarily sink in right away and, once in a while, there isn't any subsequent transformation in my outlook or behavior. When that happens, He sometimes provides another dream (or two or three) with a little different twist on the same subject. Here are a few of those, along with others I think you'll appreciate that haven't found their way into previous chapters.

September, 1986 – Some unknown event was being held at a large outdoor carnival-like setting. Throngs of people were milling around, mostly dressed like stereotypical hippies of the '60s and it was obvious that many of them were tripping. I was wary of getting close to them because we were not coming from the same reality and mingling could prove dangerous. Drawn to a stage where a performance was about to start, I noticed several special effects with lighting being used to create a perfect planetarium-like twilight sky. Near the horizon soft hues of lavender and peach and gold enhanced the ambiance of the sky's tranquility and beauty. Thousands of tiny twinkling stars were starting to come out, too, and it made me want to stay there, rather than continue to explore all there was available to see. Suddenly something went wrong and things quickly got out of hand. People were panicking and angry and became loud and unruly and all the lights became fluorescent and harsh. A group of threatening-looking young men stood nearby, all dressed in black leather. They saw me and noticed when I closed my eyes to shut out everything that was turning scary and grotesque. For some reason they took offense that I wasn't taking in all the chaos. Danger was imminent. I grabbed my purse and jacket and was about to fly up above them, out of their reach, an escape I'd used in other dreams. Sometimes that tactic worked well, other times, not well enough. Here, for the first time, I found myself yelling out Baba's name for help. "Sathya Sai Baba! Sathya Sai Baba!" I shouted at the top of my lungs. As though a rocket engine was strapped to me, I blasted off with power and speed and had a lift-off like I'd *never, EVER* experienced before! All danger was behind me in a millisecond. As I opened my eyes out of this dream, the momentum of it was still with me. "WOW! IT WORKS!" Relying on the name of God for help and protection is a tool that's available *and* powerful! The challenge is to remember to use it when I need Him.

October, 1986 – Preface: Shortly after having an epiphany, Baba showed me how the same tool could help me cope with a different kind of long-time challenge. As we already know, He confirms the old adage, *You are what you eat*. If a person eats the flesh of an animal, he or she is taking in the subtle energy of it, too, and that is not readily eliminated from the body. So, to help move forward on a spiritual track, the body, as well as the heart and mind, needs to become more purified. This, in part, means being vegetarian. I hadn't eaten chicken in ages, but I was *so* in the mood for oven-roasted chicken that day, the way my mother cooked it. Chicken (and other fowl) was my non-vegetarian Achilles heel. Giving in to the craving, I made it for dinner for myself and the family. We all savored it, with no regrets. Later that night, though, guilt set in as I thought about Baba. A huge expanse of dark space seemed to separate us. I hate that feeling, untethered and alone. Suddenly, a flash of understanding popped into my head. Growing up, the words "I love you" weren't said aloud, but it was

181

expressed and felt through the food that was made and shared. For the first time I saw the direct correlation I'd made subconsciously between them. As much as enjoying the flavor of the food, I craved the love that was also naturally infused into these home-cooked meals. If I'm not making and partaking in those foods, I'm not giving or receiving as much love as I could. Yes, I need to exert more self-discipline in this area, but now I can see that my failure to abstain from certain foods isn't solely due to willfulness and weakness. I had to figure out how to emotionally accept that I can be fulfilled and pass on love through my being, without necessarily taking it in and passing it on through food.

In this dream I'd recently returned from Disney World (which was true in real life). Instead of being home, I was near my parents' house in Auburn and found myself on a wild ride that I'd avoided when we were at the amusement park. I was by myself in a tiny open cart on a train track that took me through double doors into total blackness. It was a rollercoaster! I've never actually been on one before because the panicky feeling of nausea and a fear-induced adrenaline rush is not my idea of fun. This cart turned me completely upside down and round and round in small circles. The speed of it caused a rush of wind on my face, along with the certainty that I was going to vomit. Besides being terrified, I found myself irritated, too. I thought, *I didn't do this in Disney World, just to end up stuck on it here in Auburn?!* Desperate to make it stop, I cried out Baba's name until the cart came to an abrupt halt. Stunned and relieved and grateful all at once, I got off immediately and was safe, shaken but unharmed. This dream left me with a certainty that it was time to separate the tangled strands of love, food and family. Although it might not seem like they needed to be separated, this emotional attachment was a spiritual roadblock and posed a significant health risk to me.

April, 1994 – Preface: Before this dream occurred, I was with my mother, who'd invited me to join her on a business/pleasure trip to Paris. We were keeping up a pretty hectic pace and had decided to catch a little nap at the hotel before our evening dinner engagement. Mom fell into a deep sleep immediately. I couldn't though, because of the (never-before heard) unbelievable Donald Duck-like snores coming out of her! It was one of those *"what's wrong with this picture?"* moments, somehow so out of character and unexpected, it's hysterically funny. I couldn't stop the spontaneous belly laughs that kept erupting, to the point of tears.

At dinner that evening, others at our table ordered the roasted Duck l'orange and (since I was on vacation and saw how tempting it looked as it went by me to another table) I ordered it, too. It was as delicious and satisfying as it looked and brought about only the tiniest twinge of guilt. I hadn't heard from Baba in a while; maybe He wouldn't even notice.

Later, back at our fully booked hotel, I took a drastic measure (in my mother's eyes) to ensure I'd get some sleep that night. The size of our room only accommodated two twin-sized beds, but our bathroom was enormous. So, amid my mother's voiced concerns about my sanity, I dragged my mattress and bedding into the bathroom, to have a door between us so I might be able to get some sleep, too. (The next morning she ordered me to return it to the bedroom and arrange it back onto the box spring... so the maid wouldn't think we're crazy...) As I slept there on the bathroom floor, Baba suddenly appeared and stood in front of me, hands on His hips, looking mildly irritated and definitely exasperated. Even in the dream I remembered that I'd eaten the duck for dinner. I asked Him if He was mad at me. His complete response came in the form of one question. "Do *YOU* want to quack like a duck, *TOO*?" (*Oh no! Busted!*) Once again He made it clear that no matter where I am or what I'm doing, He *ALWAYS* KNOWS!

December, 1987 – In this dream Michael and I were home together when Baba unexpectedly arrived. We were surprised and excited that He'd come for a visit. I wanted to be a good host but wasn't prepared for His arrival in terms of food, so we invited Him to be our guest at a 'fine dining' restaurant for dinner. In a gentle, melodic voice, He ordered a simple salad for His meal. I don't know why but, along with Michael, I chose a shrimp entrée, ignoring that it wasn't vegetarian. With Michael and me taking the lead, we all engaged in pleasant 'small-talk'. Suddenly I remembered that I needed His spiritual advice on something vitally important. Dinner, however, was over by then and Baba was leaving our table, walking on ahead with other people towards the door, while I finished up, taking care of the check. By the time I was able to catch up to the group, He was gone. "NOOOOO!!!" I was crushed. I hadn't made good use of our time together; we had no meaningful conversation! A piece of metal was handed over to me by someone, as per Baba's instructions. It was a bent wire, what you would see inside a raw turkey to hold its legs together. On each end there was a rubber nipple, a baby pacifier. The message was glaring and like a slap in the face. Baba thinks I'm still in the infancy stage when I act as though *this* food (non-vegetarian) is where my source of sustenance comes from. When will I let it go? I would have sworn that we were together for just a short time, but suddenly I was in my van and pressed the 'time-elapsed' button. It showed that we'd been together for the last twenty-three hours! Impossible! Shocked and devastated that I'd wasted so much potentially precious time with meaningless small-talk, the message blared at me: *STOP WASTING TIME AND DO WHAT NEEDS TO BE DONE!* The time we have together in this life is going much faster than I'd realized! It's important to implement the changes that will help me make progress *right now!*

July, 1992 – Preface: We'd all had a hectic and exhausting day and neither Michael nor I felt like cooking, so we took the kids out for dinner. I'd been doing well for a long time in maintaining my vegetarian status. At the restaurant we both ordered the salad bar but at the last minute Michael added on some barbequed chicken, so I did, too (as if his decision gave me permission). Between being tired and hungry, I just wasn't up for fighting the urge to eat the chicken. Besides, I hadn't heard a word from Baba in more than two months; it didn't seem like I was His focal point at the moment.

In this brief dream Baba was giving a private interview to just a few *special* people (the *really* good ones!). A friend told me that he could get me in. I had my doubts. Again, even in the dream I remembered that I'd just eaten chicken and was feeling totally unworthy of being in Baba's presence. It was a pretty safe bet that He

186

wasn't happy with me right now. This friend assured me there would be no problem. All I had to do was follow right behind him. He actually scooted in. Just as I got to the doorway, however, Baba appeared and stood in my way, blocking the entrance. Sadly, looking directly into my eyes, He shook His head no, over and over. His only utterance was, "Uh-u-uhhh." It didn't take much to get the message. I had 'fowled' myself again and was not pure enough to gain admittance. Uugghh!

November, 2000 – Preface: Once while staying in the ashram, I heard our roommate's friend from Jakarta say that when Baba gives you a great amount of attention or other gifts, watch out! It's to help fortify you for an upcoming terrible and difficult challenge.

In this dream Michael and I were both at darshan in Baba's ashram. Baba came out and His energy was exceptionally powerful and serious. He came straight over to me and handed over a double-wide zip-lock baggie of vibhuti (which, in real life, I've never seen). Then He said something wonderful and reassuring, like, "Don't worry, I'll take care of you." After that, He told me, "Take padnamascar." (It's a gift of absorbing His energy through your hands by touching His feet). I did and felt a strong current-like transfer of energy, more than I ever had before. Why was He giving me all this? Nothing came to mind

187

regarding anything I'd done to deserve it. Then there was one final gift. Baba handed me a rectangular palm-sized device that was icy cold, and I knew He'd brought it to me from His own freezer, to help me stay cool. He knows how hard it is for me to handle the heat. All these acts of thoughtful generosity were great but confusing. Then the thought struck me, *Oh, no! Is something terrible going to happen?* With that, the dream ended. Afterthought: Although not officially diagnosed until more than a year later, this is when I became diabetic. With my phobia connected to needles, it's been an enormous and traumatic challenge to self-inject insulin several times a day, every day.

March, 2002 – The setting of this dream was inside the perimeter of the ashram, outdoors, but away from others. There were no sidewalks and I was standing alone on uneven and what I knew to be unstable ground. Darshan was over and I'd missed it, but all of a sudden Baba was walking towards me from a distance. The look on His face showed that there was something serious on His mind. When He arrived in front of me He pointedly said, "Food. One meal a day, dinner." I didn't know what He was talking about. "Pardon?" I asked. He repeated the sentence, just as clearly but more slowly. I thought, *I'd better write this down so I don't forget.* The dream then ended. In real life I didn't heed His advice. I love to cook and with all the cooking for family and friends that I do, following this instruction would not only be hard, I didn't see the purpose of it. Much later in hindsight, I realized that Baba gave me this instruction as a warning shortly before I was diagnosed with diabetes. If I'd listened to Him, could its onset have been prevented? This dream reinforces the fact that Baba does not interfere with free will. He offers guidance and warnings but the choice to trust and heed them is always mine.

December, 2004 – There was a group of Baba devotees all milling around in a school cafeteria, waiting for Baba to arrive. When He entered the room everyone wanted to be close and have a chance to speak to Him personally, so they queued up in a line which wrapped around the whole inside perimeter of the cafeteria. I noticed my friend, Sheela, was standing right next to Baba and would be the first to receive His attention and have a conversation with Him. There were a couple of other people who'd inconspicuously wandered over to stand next to Sheela, clearly hoping to butt in. Instead of going to the end of the long line to wait my turn, I also strolled over to join them at the head of the line. Baba didn't acknowledge any of us except Sheela, and they engaged in lively conversation and she had a wonderful darshan. When they finished, she stepped aside to make room for the next person in line. Baba continued to ignore us and gave all His attention to those who were in line. The dream ended and there was no mistaking this message: If I want Baba's attention, I'd better do what's right and get in line!

December, 2001 – Preface: I'd like to point out that Baba gave me this dream about a year before His instruction to "Pass it on!" As you've probably surmised, writing this book has proven to be the biggest seva of my life. In this dream scenario I was in the back of a packed house of a huge auditorium, waiting with everyone else for Baba to arrive to give His darshan. We were all standing rather than sitting in our seats. As soon as He came out I noticed Him say something to His assistant, and then through a hand signal, Sheela was summoned to come forward to the stage. I admired her exquisite flowy chiffon gown, which was the same shade of bright orange as Baba's robe. She and Baba were so in sync. I've never known anyone who does more seva than Sheela. It was no surprise that Baba called her first. I was also dressed in orange but the shade wasn't nearly as bright or beautiful. I couldn't help but compare myself to her and knew that I fell short from a spiritual standpoint. *But*, I thought, *at least I'm in the same family of color*. When she made her way to the front, Baba didn't immediately acknowledge her, and with the crowd pushing to get closer, she was actually squeezed back several rows, so she didn't make it onto the stage immediately.

This darshan had a different format. Rather than everyone remaining in place, Baba was allowing each person to come up to Him on stage, one at a time. So the entire audience was slowly inching its way forward towards Him. Even though Sheela and I had seats in different sections, we suddenly found ourselves both standing next to Baba at the same time. He spoke to her first about her progress on a project and appeared satisfied with what she had to report. Then He turned to me, expectantly. I didn't know what to say. I didn't have any projects or ideas or anything to update Him on. It was awkward and uncomfortable as it became increasingly obvious that I'd been sorely remiss in doing seva. Grasping at straws for anything positive to say about myself, I piped up, "I'm Italian!" I'd heard that Baba had said that Italians tend to have very good karma – abundantly compassionate, loving, hard-working and family-oriented. (I didn't mention that I'm *third* generation Italian... I was looking for Brownie points.) Just after informing Him of my heritage, a more *authentic* Italian woman showed up on stage next to me, who'd arrived straight from Italy! *(Uh-oh!)* She'd brought along a big power-point presentation for Baba to see the results of her ambitious, wide scope seva project. *Oh God...*

The scene shifted and there was a group of us, including Baba, Sheela, and myself in someone's kitchen. As a gift from our host, we'd been invited over for a big home-made feast. The mouth-watering aromas in the air reminded me of Thanksgiving. While we were all standing around companionably chatting, someone else walked in, informing us that our host's mother wanted us to go to her house to eat instead. The meal, however, was already prepared and just about ready to be served in the house we were in. Looking around in the kitchen, I could see how much time and effort had gone into its preparation and knew that this food was a special gift of love; our host intended to give us her best. No one else spoke up to respond, so I did, decisively declining. It wouldn't be right to accommodate our host's mother, even if she did normally command more clout. If we left at this point, all the work our host had done would be wasted, as well as the opportunity for everyone to enjoy this terrific meal. The dream then ended.

Afterthought: In the first part, the message was obvious (and not the first one I've had on this topic). There's no point in judging and comparing myself to anyone else. Yes, Sheela was dressed in the identical shade of Baba's robe, while my color was 'off' and less impressive, but that isn't indicative of my value. Even though it looked like she would be standing next to Baba first, it actually turned out that Sheela and I were both in the same proximity to Him at the same time. Although she'd already accomplished a great deal and I didn't have a clue as to what I should be doing, it didn't change my 'nearness' to Baba. There is no competition when it comes to spirituality. Apparently, I needed to be reminded of the importance of seva, though. Between what I've read and experienced, offering selfless, compassionate help to others is the fastest way to remove egotistical tendencies and to serve God. It benefits the recipient, the giver, and I think it makes God smile, too.

Understanding the symbology of the kitchen scenario eluded me for years but I think it's finally come to light. I never saw our host and I believe it's because I actually *was* the host, the one who'd assembled all the ingredients (experiences with Baba) in order to offer this meal (the book) as a gift to others.(Profits will be donated to charities.) It also escaped me that this delicious 'food' was for the soul instead of the tummy. Everyone in the kitchen realized that what we were about to partake in was special and it had been prepared lovingly from scratch. The mother of the host (someone more experienced, with an elevated status) wanted us to change plans and go to her house instead, to feed us what she chose to give. There was no question in my heart that it wouldn't be right.

Since no one else spoke up to refuse the mother's instruction to walk out on what was about to be served, I felt compelled to defend the host and the meal. Although she wasn't a professional chef (credentialed author), her feast was still worthy of being enjoyed and appreciated. A great deal of effort had been expended and it was all just about done (down on paper), organic and unprocessed (real and healthy) and ready to be served (published).

The mother's lack of concern for the host's efforts and apparent dismissal of what she had to offer was daunting (and not unfamiliar to me) but, for the first time, despite all the doubts in my ability to create this, I've come to believe that I have accomplished what Baba asked me to do. I finally think Michael was right when he told me so many years ago, "If Baba asked you to do this, He must have known that you *could* do it!"

No matter how my style and expertise might differ from others, *all this*, my background and experiences with Baba, is the kitchen and ingredients I have to work with to offer you what I can give. I hope this 'feast' of passing on Baba's love and joy and sustenance has been gratifying and fortified you. At the very least, if you wanted it, what you've been given here has satisfied your 'sweet tooth'! Just please remember, with Baba as your Executive Chef there's no limit to the spectacular, fulfilling 'meals' the two of you can create in *your* kitchen! Enjoy! Sai Ram!

# References

Baba, SSS (1975). Prema Vahini, Bangalore, India, Sri Sathya Sai Books & Publications Trust

Baba, SSS (1976). Sadhana the Inward Path, Prashanti Nilayam, Andhra Pradesh, India, Sri Sathya Sai Books & Publications Trust

Baba, SSS (1980). Sathyam Sivam Sundaram, Part IV New Delhi, India, M. Gulab Singh & Sons Pvt. Ltd.

Baba, SSS (1988). Discourses on the Bhagavad Gita, Prashanti Nilayam, Andhra Pradesh, India

Baba, SSS (1999). A Compendium of the Teachings of Sathya Sai Baba, compiled by Charlene Leslie-Chaden, Bangalore, India, Sai Towers Publishing

Baba, SSS (1999). Sathya Sai Speaks Vol. XXV, Prashanti Nilayam, Andhra Pradesh, India, Sri Sathya Sai Books & Publication Trust

Chinmayananda, S (1989). Talks on Sankara's Vivekachoodamani, Bombay, India, Central Chinmaya Mission Trust

Hislop, JS (1985). My Baba & I, Ann Arbor, MI, Birth Day Publishing Co.

Murphet, H (1971). Sai Baba Man of Miracles, York Beach, ME, Samuel Weiser, Inc.

Organ, TW (1970). The Hindu Quest for the Perfection of Man, Athens, OH. Ohio University